EVERYTHING

YOU NEED TO KNOW ABOUT...

Becoming a Father

EVERYTHING

YOU NEED TO KNOW ABOUT...

Becoming a Father

KEVIN NELSON

D&C

David and Charles

A DAVID & CHARLES BOOK
David & Charles is a subsidiary of F+W (UK) Ltd.,
an F+W Publications Inc. company

First published in the UK in 2005
First published in the USA as The Everything® Father-To-Be Book,
by Adams Media in 2004

A catalogue record for this book is available from the British Library.

ISBN 0 7153 2318 0

Printed in Great Britain by CPI Bath
for David & Charles
Brunel House   Newton Abbot   Devon

Visit our website at www.davidandcharles.co.uk

David & Charles books are available from all good bookshops;
alternatively you can contact our Orderline on (0)1626 334555 or
write to us at FREEPOST EX2110, David & Charles Direct,
Newton Abbot, TQ12 4ZZ (no stamp required UK only).

Contents

Acknowledgments / ix
Top Ten Things Every Father-to-Be Should Know / x
Introduction / xi

1 The New World of Fatherhood / 1
Becoming a Father 2 · Greater Expectations, Greater Rewards 3 · Birth Then and Now 5 · Dad as Labour Partner 6 · A Different Role for You 8 · The Changes Ahead 9

2 Conception and Pregnancy / 11
Planned and Unplanned 12 · Hearing the News 12 · Your Job Begins: Reassuring Her 14 · The Home Pregnancy Test 15 · Seeing the Midwife 16 · Looking Ahead to the Due Date 17 · What Happens Now? 18 · Sharing the News 19 · Early Workplace Strategies 21

3 Riding the Pregnancy Roller Coaster / 25
The Stages of Pregnancy 26 · Morning Sickness 29 · Cravings 30 · Her Changing Body 31 · Sympathy Pains 32 · A Volatile Issue: Her Weight 33 · The Emotional Roller Coaster 36

4 Doctors and Medical Tests / 39
What's Involved? 40 · The Obstetrician 40 · Antenatal Doctor Visits 42 · Monitoring Progress 43 · Ultrasound Scans 44 · Boy or Girl? 46 · Surprise! It's Twins! 48 · Amniocentesis and CVS 50 · Threat of Miscarriage 51

5 Your Suddenly Expanding Family / 55
Your Shifting Social World 56 · Her Family 57 · Your Family 60 · Accepting Help 61 · Feelings of Isolation 62 · Coping Strategies 63

6

Common Fears / 67

Your Feelings Are Normal 68 · Passing Out in the Delivery Room 68 · Not Being Able to Provide 69 · Is It Really My Child? 71 · Ageing and Mortality 71 · Becoming like Dad 73 · Will My Relationship Be Hurt? 75 · Concerns about Your Partner 76 · Concerns about the Baby 76 · Getting Support 77

7

The Economics of Having a Baby / 81

Money Worries 82 · Money: It's a Family Affair 83 · The Emotions of Money 84 · Setting Your Priorities 86 · Strategies for Getting Money 86 · Baby Expenses 89 · Getting Help 90

8

Long-Term Financial Issues / 93

Why Your Perspective Is Valuable 94 · Buying a Bigger Vehicle 94 · Owning a Home 96 · Life Insurance 98 · Making a Will 100 · Saving for Education 100 · Thinking about Retirement 101

9

Job, Work, Career / 103

Your Role as Provider 104 · Planning for When the Baby Comes 104 · Steps to Take at Work 106 · Paternity Leave 107 · Other Job Options 110 · Her Job and Workplace 111 · Gender Roles 112 · Getting a Better Job 113 · Working from Home 115

10

Health: Yours, Hers and the Baby's / 117

Leading the Way 118 · Alcohol 118 · Cigarette Smoking 120 · Recreational and Over-the-Counter Drugs 122 · Eating Healthily 122 · Developing Healthy Habits 124 · Cooking 125 · Exercise 127 · Her Need for Rest 128

11

Sex During Pregnancy / 129

Sex and the Pregnant Father 130 · Understanding Your Partner 130 · Your Attitude 132 · Will Sex Hurt the Baby? 134 · Holding and Cuddling 136 · Finding a Comfortable Position 137 · Towards a New Intimacy 139

12

Making Sound Decisions / 141

Speak Up: It's Your Child, Too 142 · Naming the Little One 143 · How Much Do We Tell Other People? 145 · Home Birth versus Hospital 146 · Having the Birth You Both Want 148 · Writing a Birth Plan 148 · Birth Control 150 · Nappies 151

13

Preparing Your Home and Car / 153

The Nesting Instinct 154 · Preparing the Nursery 155 · The Family Bed 157 · Babyproofing Your Home 158 · In the Event of an Emergency 159 · Staying in Touch: Mobile Phones 161 · Car Seats 162

14

Birthing Partner / 165

What a Birthing Partner Does 166 · Antenatal Classes 168 · Supporting Mum Physically 168 · Providing Emotional Support 170 · The Hospital Visit 170 · What to Bring to the Hospital 172 · Asking a Family Member to Assist You 174 · Hiring a Birth Attendant 174

15

The Big Day Arrives / 177

Getting Labour Started 178 · The Stages of Labour 179 · Early Signs of Progress 181 · Keeping Early Labour Moving Along 182 · Things You Need to Do 183 · The Best Place for Early Labour 186 · The Drive to the Hospital 187

16

Labour and Delivery / 189

Admission 190 · 'Nothing Much Is Happening' 191 · Delivery Room Procedures 192 · The Birth Team 193 · When Labour Stalls 195 · Pain Relief Options 196 · Pushing 198 · Congratulations! You're a Father! 198 · The Placenta 200

17 Real-Life Birth Scenarios / 201

Expect the Unexpected 202 · Premature Birth 203 · Emergency Roadside Delivery 204 · Medical Intervention 205 · Baby Is Late 206 · Caesarean Delivery 207 · Being a Birth Partner at a Caesarean Birth 208 · Recovery from a Caesarean 210 · Trusting Your Instincts (and Hers) 211

18 The Immediate Aftermath / 213

Taking a Moment with Your New Family 214 · Baby Health Checks 214 · Letting Everyone Know 215 · Other Jobs and Responsibilities 217 · Meeting Siblings 219 · Taking Pictures 219 · Shooting with a Camcorder 220 · Celebrating the Arrival 222 · Taking Mother and Baby Home 222

19 Baby Comes Home / 225

So What Do We Do Now? 226 · Introducing Baby to Your Pet 226 · Supporting Your Family 228 · The Breastfeeding Challenge 229 · Helping Out Around the House 232 · Caring for Your Child 232 · Getting Rest 236 · Emotional Highs and Lows 236

20 What's Ahead for You and Your Family / 239

Surviving the First Months 240 · The Work–Family Balance 240 · Exploring Other Options 242 · Finding Childcare 243 · The Battle for Sleep 245 · Time and Money Pressures 247 · You and Your Partner 247 · You and Your Baby 249 · Remembering to Enjoy 251

Appendix A · Suggested Reading for New Fathers / **254**
Appendix B · Websites for Fathers / **255**
Index / **257**

Acknowledgments

Many people helped me with this book. First, I wish to thank my wife Jennifer and my three children, who make me a better man. Being a husband and a father are the best things I have ever done in my life.

I also wish to thank my editor Eric M. Hall, who has shown extraordinary patience with me, and Gene Brissie, who, in addition to being my agent, is a good friend.

Last but not least, I owe a debt of gratitude to another good friend, Max Lateiner, who let me stay briefly in his house while I was deeply involved in writing this book. After living the bachelor life with Max for a couple of days, it made coming home to a houseful of screaming, crying kids seem positively sane in comparison.

Top Ten Things
Every Father-to-Be Should Know

1. How to keep your sex life thriving, active and fun during pregnancy.

2. What to say – and what not to say – about your partner's changing body and other pregnancy issues.

3. How to be the world's greatest labour partner.

4. How to keep your sanity when the in-laws and other family members descend on you.

5. The inside knowledge on how and when to share the news with your boss and colleagues.

6. Why you can relax about fainting in the delivery room (it won't really happen).

7. Tips on how to balance your work and job with your new responsibilities as a father.

8. How to be a hero to your partner when she's feeling low, ill or scared.

9. How to cope with all the changes that are occurring in your life.

10. How to minimize the stress and maximize the enjoyment of having a baby.

Introduction

THE WRITER DAVID BLANKENHORN has remarked that being a father is the most important thing most men will ever do in their lives. Only a few select individuals will get the chance to be prime minister or to rescue a stranded family from a burning building or shoot the winning goal in the FA Cup Final. But many men will become fathers, giving them the opportunity to become everyday heroes to their children.

This book is intended for new fathers and fathers-to-be. It is designed to guide the new father through the ups and downs of pregnancy, taking him all the way through to the birth of his child and the day he brings his son or daughter home for the first time. While the focus is on first-timers, there is plenty of good information here for second- and third-time fathers who may need a refresher course on how to be a labour partner and other issues related to having a baby.

Many men are not sure what to think when they learn, for the first time, that they are going to become a father. Panic is one reaction. Another is, 'How can this be happening to me?' After the initial anxiety passes, many new fathers really get into the idea. They become curious about this new thing they have never experienced, and they want to learn more.

Not all new fathers are like this, of course. Some are more reluctant participants. Because the baby is developing inside their partner's body, not theirs, they may feel uninvolved or cut off from what's going on. These men may have to go through the birth itself and see the baby before they finally feel connected to the drama that has been unfolding around them for the previous nine months. The goal of this book is to speak to all types of new fathers – those who are into it and involved from the outset, and those who may need a little nudging here and there.

Men tend to be mission-orientated. Give us a mission or a job, and we will go out and do it. The problem that some new fathers have with pregnancy is that they are not sure what to do or what their job is. This book will show you the jobs that you can do during this time, including, most importantly perhaps, how you can support your partner.

Ah, but there's the rub. This may be an unfamiliar position for many men. They may not be accustomed to playing second fiddle in their family. But childbirth is fundamentally about two people: Mum and baby. While important in the overall scheme of things, Dad must learn to accept a secondary, supporting role.

Nothing physical happens inside the body of the man during pregnancy (although some do feel sympathy pains when their partners are going through morning sickness). And yet he is being asked to make the journey from not being a father to being a father. Is it any wonder that some men stumble along the way? Fathers-to-be experience emotions they've never had before – fears of fainting in the delivery room, worry about the health of the baby, financial worries, concern over how a child will affect their relationship with their partner – and they're not quite sure how to deal with them. Some are embarrassed that they have these emotions at all.

To be prepared, when an adventurer explores uncharted terrain, he takes a compass and map with him. For new fathers and their partners, pregnancy is a trip into a vast, unexplored territory. As you find your way, let this book serve as your compass and map.

Chapter 1

The New World of Fatherhood

It is a brand-new world for fathers today. Becoming a father today is a far different enterprise than it was for your father when you were born. These changes bring greater challenges and responsibilities for men, but they also offer immense rewards and joys. This chapter will prepare you for the road ahead and what to expect along the way.

Becoming a Father

To state the obvious, being a father is different from being a mother. You have a different role in the family and a different job to do. You see things differently from your partner. And you will have a different relationship with your child from the one she has.

Some of the most crucial differences between a father and a mother become obvious during pregnancy. The most dramatic, and visible, changes occur with the woman. Her body changes as the baby grows inside her. Along with these physical changes comes a whole host of emotions.

A father, on the other hand, is an entirely different animal. Although some men experience sympathy pains and other physical symptoms, virtually nothing happens directly to the man. His body does not expand and change. He's the same person he always was – except that now he is about to have a little rug rat crawling around the house. Help!

The Internet is a boundless source of information that can help to answer specific questions that arise. Some of this information is reliable; some is not. On medical issues involving pregnancy, it is always best to follow a midwife or doctor's advice and your own common sense, rather than any advice you may find on the Internet.

The unique challenge that men face is that they must come to terms with becoming a father almost entirely on an emotional level, rather than a physical one. But the good news today for fathers-to-be is that they have an unprecedented level of support and a wide variety of resources available to them. Some of those resources include the following:

· This book and others like it that are written for men
· Fatherhood and parenting websites on the Internet
· Chat groups on the Internet
· Other fathers
· Men's and fathers' support groups
· Partners and families

These and other resources are potentially useful to men, and they are discussed in greater detail later in this book. It is important for new fathers to realize that they are not alone as they embark on this journey.

Greater Expectations, Greater Rewards

Today, more is expected of fathers than ever before. You are expected to be a good provider, but that is not all. You are also expected to actively participate in the birth of your child and to take a hands-on approach in raising him or her. Additionally, your partner expects you to always be there for her in a loving, nurturing way.

It's a lot to handle, isn't it? At times it may seem overwhelming. But fatherhood is a job, and, like any job, it helps to know what your responsibilities are and how you fit in. Here, then, is a general job description for being a father.

Job One: Provider/Protector

Despite all the ways that fatherhood has changed over the years, your primary role is the same as it was for the cavemen and for every father since then. You need to provide for your family, and it's your job to protect them to make sure they are safe. The mother's primary focus will be inwards, on the baby. Yours will be on creating a safe, secure place to raise your child.

Men are hard-wired for this job. It is not something that you will need to go to college to learn. Often the first thoughts a man has when he learns his partner is pregnant are these: 'How am I going to pay for this? Do I need to work more? What do I need to do to make this happen?'

All men have these thoughts or similar ones. They are normal and natural, an instinctive reaction to the promise and responsibility of childbirth. Being a good provider is the most fundamental way you can help your partner and child.

Job Two: Participant

One of the biggest jobs a father has is as a labour partner – a responsibility that will be discussed in greater detail later. But being a labour partner is only one aspect of a larger requirement for fathers today. They are expected to participate in all areas of family and household life. This is in part due to the fact that a great many women are themselves working outside the home, and these mothers need more help with the baby from their partners.

Being asked to participate more may seem like a negative at first. You feel as if you are being pulled in many directions at the same time. But it can be a positive. With greater responsibilities come greater rewards. Since you are around your child more – changing nappies, feeding her, taking her for walks – you develop a closer relationship with her. And what father doesn't want that?

Birth and health-care specialists say that one of the biggest worries of fathers-to-be is that they will faint during their child's birth. Many men have seen films or television shows in which the father collapses comically in the delivery room. But in fact, these experts say, this almost never happens.

Job Three: Support Person and Nurturer

A vital part of being a father is supporting your partner. By supporting her, you support your child. Having a good relationship with your partner is the best thing the two of you can do for your child. Some fathers-to-be may be uncomfortable with this job because it represents a change in the way you perceive yourself and your role as a man. Putting your partner's needs ahead of yours is an important part of showing your commitment – to both your partner and your future child.

First and foremost, listen to your partner. Let her talk about her feelings, and try to listen without judging or criticizing. Demonstrate that she can confide in you about the sometimes scary changes that are happening inside her.

Birth Then and Now

People have been having babies since – well, since the beginning of people. But the childbirth process has changed dramatically over the years. These changes have largely come about through advances in medical technology that make it safer than ever before to have a baby. Although there are still risks in childbirth, for both the mother and the baby, there are significantly fewer risks than previous generations had to contend with.

The Way It Used to Be

For centuries, almost all births took place at home. Childbirth was regarded as the exclusive domain of women. Usually only females were present, including a midwife who assisted in the delivery. Fathers rarely participated, nor were they expected to.

The mortality rate was far higher than it is today. Sometimes the baby, or the mother, died during childbirth. Because it involved creation, the act of having a child was imbued with mystery. Ritual and superstition entered into it, and the midwife, who was rarely if ever medically trained, often oversaw these rites.

Childbirth as a Medical Procedure

In more recent generations, the hospital replaced the home as the primary place to have a baby. Anaesthesia came into use, which required a doctor's involvement. Additionally, people began to feel that a hospital with doctors, nurses and trained medical specialists on hand was the best environment for both mother and child.

Once hospitals and doctors got into the act, the process of having a baby underwent a major transformation. Where it had once been seen as a very natural act of creation, childbirth was now viewed as a medical procedure similar to surgery. Mum was, in fact, placed on a surgical table, her feet resting in stirrups. She received medication to numb the pain, and the operation proceeded. In the words of Dr William Sears, a leading birth expert, the baby was then 'extracted'.

One element of childbirth that did not change from earlier times, however, was the role of dear old Dad. Just as in earlier days, he was the odd man out. Most of the time you could find him in the waiting room, nervously pacing the floor. When the baby arrived, he brought flowers to Mum (still not a bad idea) and poured the drinks.

When you discuss pregnancy-related issues with your partner, remember that you do not have to decide everything today. The goal is to find common ground. Keep it all in perspective. After the health and safety of your baby and partner, everything else is just detail.

Birth Today

The experience of giving birth today is not how it was for your parents or grandparents. Hospitals and their labour and delivery procedures have changed in recent decades. In part, this is a response to couples who have insisted on more involvement for the father and less of a 'surgical' feel to the birth experience.

You will, of course, want the best doctors, midwives and medical services available to you. Even if you choose not to use it in every case, you will probably like the idea of having the latest technology at your disposal, especially if a crisis occurs. And you will want information about all your options, including pain-killing drugs (again, even if your partner opts not to use them).

But if you are like nearly all couples these days, you want your child's birth to be more than a purely medical event. Some couples may decide not to have their baby in a hospital but rather at home. Those at a hospital nevertheless want to birth their baby in a setting that resembles home – a place that is quiet, comfortable and relaxed. Whatever 'blend' of old and new you and your partner choose, the two of you are sure to be making lots of decisions over the next months – more decisions, perhaps, than you have ever made together before.

Dad as Labour Partner

Not so long ago, fathers were left completely out of the picture during birth. But that has changed radically. From the onset of pregnancy to birth and beyond, this generation of fathers is more actively involved with their children than any other in history.

An overwhelming percentage of fathers serve as 'birth coach' for their partner. They look forward to this challenge and rise to the responsibilities it entails. Giving birth is not a 'woman's matter' any more. Men accept that they are part of the equation, too, and for the most part they are happy to be one of the first faces welcoming their babies into the world.

In the UK, statutory paternity entitlement is two weeks' paid leave after your baby is born. To qualify, you must be the biological father of the baby or the mother's husband or partner, and expect to be responsible for bringing up the child. You need to have been employed by your present employer for 26 weeks by the 15th week before the date of childbirth. You don't have to take your leave immediately after the birth – you can take it whenever you like, as long as it is completed by the 56th day after your baby is born. Unlike maternity leave, you can't start your leave before the birth.

Some fathers report a negative attitude from the medical profession, which does not help to alleviate your own feelings of uncertainty and possible incompetence. You may not feel comfortable in a medical setting. You may not understand everything about a woman's body, and your questions may seem crude and stupid. All this may make you wonder if you are up to the task ahead.

You owe it to at least three people to fight through the negativity and doubts and keep going. The first is your partner, who needs you by her side. The second is your growing child, who, it has been shown, learns to distinguish his mother's and father's voices while still in the womb. Last but not least is you. Being present for the birth of your child is without doubt one of the most amazing experiences you will ever have.

A Different Role for You

While being a labour partner is important, it is nonetheless secondary to the bigger job that your partner is doing. She is the one who is giving birth to the baby and doing the real, painful work. Seeing their partners going through so much agony, most men are glad not to be in that position.

Still, it points out a central fact: you are not the central player in this drama. Baby and Mum come first, and you are a distant third. This may be an unfamiliar position for you. But being a father in today's world means that you must learn and adapt to new roles for yourself.

A Supporting Role

As mentioned, you are not the lead actor in this drama; your partner and baby are. The job of a supporting actor is just that – to support the leading players. Your job is essentially to make the star of the show – the mother of your child – feel good and keep her performing. If you do that, you will be doing your job.

In the later months of pregnancy, you will be offered antenatal classes together. These classes focus principally on Mum. As her partner, you are there essentially to learn techniques to support her, physically and emotionally, when she goes into labour. Again, this is a valuable role – but still a supporting one.

An Advisory Role

One of the vital roles that a man plays during pregnancy, and especially during childbirth, is that of advisor. You are going to advise your partner on lots of things. Some advice she will heed; some of it she will ignore.

Ultimately, though, your partner will make the final call, not you. Most men accept this and have no problem with it. They trust her instincts, especially in matters concerning her own body, and are willing to play second fiddle in this situation.

A Decision-Making Role

In the throes of labour, however, a woman may be unable to make decisions for herself. She may be out of her mind with pain. That is where you sometimes have to step in; assess the situation based on the advice of doctors, midwives and others; and make tough, on-the-spot decisions.

These decisions affect not only you, but your partner and your baby, too. Whatever role you happen to be playing at any given moment, when you make a decision, you will now have to consider its impact on your family. Get used to it. That is what it means to be a father.

The responsibility for making decisions during labour and delivery never falls solely on the shoulders of the birth partner. Doctors and midwives are there to advise, and they can and will intervene if necessary. You can also hire a private midwife to give you advice and support.

The Changes Ahead

It is true what they say: having a baby changes everything. These changes reach into all the major departments of your life – and the minor ones too. And these changes begin virtually as soon as you hear her say, 'Um, guess what? I think I've missed my period.'

There is no reason to panic when you hear these words. Just pick yourself up off the floor and start making plans for the changes that lie ahead. Generally speaking, you can expect changes in three key areas of your life.

Your Relationship

Changes may have already occurred in this department, depending on how far along your partner is in her pregnancy. She may have less time and attention for you. She may not have as much interest in sex as she once did. She may be extremely tired or experiencing morning sickness. She may be riding an emotional roller coaster that you have trouble keeping up with at times.

There's no denying that a baby (even one still in the womb) creates stresses and strains on a couple. But when both parties are willing, this time is also a golden opportunity to grow together as a couple.

Your Job and Career

Changes will most certainly occur in the professional realm, too, once you find out you're having a baby. Both you and your employer may suddenly regard each other in a different light.

For example, you may work long hours or travel frequently in your job. But with a baby on the way, you may not want to be away quite so much from your partner. And when the baby comes, you may want to be at home even more. Your changed view towards your job may in turn cause your employer to reassess your place and standing in the company.

 Studies have shown that becoming a father can help a man in his work life. Feeling the need to provide for his family, he works harder, which spurs him on to greater accomplishments and a better career. Having a baby also teaches patience, perseverance and other lessons that improve job performance.

Your View of the World

The biggest change in your life when you become a father is the change that occurs in your outlook. Your attitude about things, your view of the world, shifts and expands. You no longer look at things in quite the same way you did before.

This change in attitude does not occur overnight. It comes on slowly, in time. Pregnancy covers three-quarters of a year, which gives you ample time to come to terms with the idea of becoming a father.

Of course, your partner may have an entirely different view – about the length of a pregnancy, that is. She is, after all, the one who is carrying the baby around inside her. And that baby keeps growing and growing. By the ninth month or so she is going to be quite sick of the whole business and ready to not be pregnant any longer.

Becoming a father is one of the simplest things a man can do – and one of the most complicated. There are great expectations and challenges for fathers today, along with great joys and rewards.

Chapter 2

Conception and Pregnancy

Fatherhood begins at the very moment of conception. After this moment comes knowledge – the crazy, apple-cart-upsetting knowledge that, yes, you are indeed going to have a baby. What do you do when you first hear the news? What steps do you take at home and at work? This chapter gives you the lowdown.

Planned and Unplanned

The majority of pregnancies are unplanned. They come as a surprise to both Mum and Dad. Surprise may, in fact, be too mild a word. Both of you may feel at first like you were hit over the head with a cricket bat.

Conception is a simple yet mysterious process. Some couples may have been trying hard to have a baby, stopped for a while because they were unsuccessful, and then suddenly and inexplicably got pregnant. Others may have caught lightning in a bottle and conceived a child the first weekend they made love after stopping birth control. Some may have become pregnant while on the pill or another form of contraception.

Ultimately, the genesis of your pregnancy does not matter. What matters is the fact that both of you are bringing a new life into the world.

A man ejaculates from 200 to 400 million sperm during an orgasm. Only some of these sperm survive the journey up the womb to the promised land of a woman's fallopian tubes. Once a single sperm enters the egg, the door is shut and no other sperm can get in. The fusion of that single sperm with the egg forms the single cell that begins your baby's life.

Hearing the News

After he plants the seed, a man essentially loses control of the gestation process. The power, if you want to call it that, reverts to the woman. She is the one who carries the baby, the one whose internal processes will transform that single cell into a fully formed, amazingly complex tiny human being with eyes, ears, nose, lips, skin and maybe even some cute fluffy wisps of hair just like Dad's.

Your partner is also the first to know about her possible pregnancy. It does not matter whether it was planned or not. In every case, she will know or suspect that something is different before you see any signs because she will have missed her period. In some cases, she may even have proceeded without you – received confirmation of her pregnancy from a home pregnancy testing kit – before she lets you in on her secret.

This puts you into a reactive position. She is going to be telling you the news, even if it is still preliminary, and you are going to be on the receiving end. The emotions you may feel when you hear this news for the first time are worth exploring.

Shock

Learning that you are about to have a baby, if you were not expecting it, is shocking news. Even if you were planning and hoping for it, it can still catch you off guard. You may feel stunned by this news, completely blown away. 'What?' you say. 'Are you sure?'

Before fully accepting the news, many men need to see the results of a pregnancy test. A test provides outside verification beyond the simple fact that your partner may have missed her period. The possibility still exists that she is only late and that this is a false alarm. A test is a reasonable next step, and your partner will want one too, if she has not already had one.

Fear and Worry

After your immediate shock dissipates, more emotions will follow. You may feel all of these things at once, or they may come on over time. All of what you feel falls under the category of 'normal and natural' – every father-to-be experiences similar emotions at one time or another.

This is your first baby. It is the first time you have ever travelled down this road. When you do anything for the first time, the venture causes worry and perhaps a little fear. You do not know what to expect because you have never done this before. People can tell you what it is like, but that is not the same thing as actually living it and experiencing it for yourself. Until you do, these feelings of worry and unease will probably always be at the back of your mind.

Sadness

Sadness or even depression can come over you in your quieter moments after learning you are about to become a father. While a woman feels as if she is gaining something in having a child, many men experience an opposite reaction. They experience feelings of loss. You may be asking yourself, 'Is my partner going to get so wrapped up in the baby that she forgets about me? Am I going to lose her? Is having a baby going to hurt our relationship?' All of these questions and more are discussed in Chapter 6.

Excitement

Emotions, being emotions, are hard to predict. They do not follow a predictable pattern. If you do not feel these exact emotions right away, that is perfectly OK. Every man is entitled to his own emotional response; there are no 'shoulds' here. Of course, if you do not feel anything at all upon hearing the news you are going to be a father, that may mean your body is in total shock. It's a good idea to lie down somewhere until you feel better.

Be careful how you react when she breaks the news to you (although that may be easier said than done). Try not to put her on the defensive. Take a moment to gather your thoughts before responding, if you can, because you do not want to say something that will hurt her feelings.

Once you get over the initial shock, excitement is another emotion you will definitely feel at some point. It is possible, however, that your partner's initial excitement may surpass your own. She may be bubbly as champagne while you feel flat. The reverse may be true, too – you may feel elated, but she may feel as if the world just fell on top of her. And whatever is going on inside your head, you will need to deal in some way with her feelings.

Your Job Begins: Reassuring Her

It is worth noting that even in the murky world of emotions, the laws of science still apply. This is Isaac Newton's famous Third Law of Motion:

for every action, there is an equal and opposite reaction. Every careful man understands that when his partner first says those fateful words to him, 'I'm pregnant', his reaction is critical. If you are in a committed relationship with this woman and she loves you, her feelings about this surprising development in your lives will be influenced, to some degree, by what you say and how you react.

Men are not robots. You are going to have an emotional response to this breathtaking news. What may help you, however, is a little understanding of what your partner is going through at this moment. She is going to be all over the map emotionally, surging with feelings that are similar to (but still different from) yours, such as these:

- Excitement over having a baby of her own
- Worry over what you are thinking and how you may react
- Anxiety over what this may mean for your relationship
- Uncertainty because she has so many questions that need answers
- Concern that during the weeks she did not know she was pregnant, she has somehow unintentionally harmed her baby's health
- Fear about the pain of childbirth that she has heard so many stories about
- Relief that something she has perhaps wanted for some time has finally come to pass.

Emotions are coursing through both of you like a raging river. You have a great deal to talk about. These early moments can be intensely meaningful in the life of a couple, and yet they also carry potential risk. Above all, your partner needs to know that no matter what, you are in this together.

The Home Pregnancy Test

A home pregnancy test is a commercial product that can provide a preliminary assessment of whether or not your partner is bearing a child. There are several different brands available for sale at pharmacies, including those in supermarkets, for about £10. Most couples cannot resist the temptation to run down to the shop and pick one up to see if what they suspect may actually be true.

For best results, a woman should wait two or three days after her menstrual cycle has run its course to make sure she is not jumping the gun. You almost assuredly know nothing about the timing of your partner's monthly cycle. As with so many other things having to do with pregnancy, you will have to rely on her.

Your partner will almost certainly perform the test herself. It involves collecting a urine sample, and while you may see yourself as involved and supportive, you do not want to be *that* involved. When she is done, you can inspect the results together, although they are sometimes hard to read. A coloured line forms on the test strip that indicates whether or not a fertilized egg is present in the uterine wall. But this line may be very faint, and you may have to try again.

Free pregnancy tests used to be available at doctors' surgeries and family planning clinics, but they are now being phased out and most women do their own test at home. A home pregnancy test can confirm a pregnancy from as early as the first day of a missed period – in other words, just two weeks after conception. The kit is highly accurate if used properly. It works by detecting a pregnancy hormone in a woman's urine. If the hormone is present, the indicator stick changes colour, or a coloured line appears, which means she is pregnant. But while a negative result may mean your partner is not pregnant, it may simply mean that there is not yet enough pregnancy hormone in her urine to give a positive result. It's a good idea to do the test again in a few days.

Seeing the Midwife

Once your partner has had a positive pregnancy test, she should make an appointment to see one of the community midwives attached to her local doctors' practice. There, she can discuss her general health; talk about birth options and any tests she might need and when; find out about eating well and looking after herself; get advice on dealing with any pregnancy discomforts; organize a booking appointment at the hospital (if the baby is to be born in hospital) and work out the baby's due date.

The length of the pregnancy will be calculated from the first day of your partner's last menstrual period (LMP). The midwife adds nine months and seven days to the date when the last period started. However, if your partner has irregular periods or has any bleeding in early pregnancy, the LMP method probably won't be relevant; instead, she will probably be offered an ultrasound scan, which will give a good idea of the baby's due date.

The news of a baby on the way is cause for celebration. Buy your partner flowers or a gift. Treat yourselves to a special dinner, or go on an outing together to the beach or a park. Or don't do anything – just create a quiet time to sit together with the news.

Looking Ahead to the Due Date

Two questions immediately pop into the minds of most parents-to-be when they learn they are pregnant: 'Will it be a boy or girl?' and 'When will he or she arrive?'

From conception to birth, pregnancy normally lasts anywhere from thirty-seven to forty-two weeks, which, if you do the maths, is not nine months. It is more like nine months plus or even ten months. The fact is that some babies come early, and some come late. Very few of them arrive when they are supposed to or according to your carefully thought-out plans.

A due date makes the whole business of having a baby seem a little more real, especially for men. The growing embryo is immediately a real and active presence for your partner because, ready or not, changes are occurring in her body. Not so with a man. Being able to flip to a page on a calendar and note the day in July or September or January helps make the process seem a little less abstract.

Be careful, however, about revealing the date to in-laws, relatives and friends. It is better to be on the vague side – tell them the due month, perhaps, rather than the actual day. The reason for this is that if people know the date, as it gets closer and closer, they will start calling you to ask 'Any news yet?' However well-meaning they may be, you and especially your partner do not need or want that sort of pressure at that time.

Calculating the due date is an inexact science. It is done for the benefit of adults, and babies pay no attention to it. More than 90 per cent of all babies will not arrive on their due date. Most, however, are born within two weeks of the due date.

What Happens Now?

At about five or six weeks of life, the embryo inside your partner's body – your baby – is about the size of an apple pip. Despite his tiny size, he has already formed a simple brain and has begun to develop the beginnings of a spine, blood vessels and a central nervous system. His tiny heart is starting to beat. Although he has grown immensely in a very short time, he still has a long way to go before he is ready to come out.

This is a good thing – a great thing. It gives you time to absorb some of what you have been feeling. You do not need to know everything right away. You will learn what you need to know, and you can work out all the things that need to be worked out in time.

Doctors strongly urge pregnant women to stop certain habits because of their potential harm to the baby. These include smoking, drinking alcohol and using recreational drugs; they also advise cutting down drinking caffeinated beverages. Your partner should avoid taking antibiotics or over-the-counter drugs until she speaks to her doctor.

But there are some things you need to get moving on from the start. Your partner needs to start taking folic acid supplements straight away. A gentle reminder from you until she gets into the habit might be nice. She will naturally take more interest in her pregnancy than you do because it directly affects her body. Because of her self-interest, instincts and passion, and because you may not feel entirely comfortable discussing female body issues, you may be inclined to step back and let her take charge. This strategy works well enough up to a point. A better approach is to show support for your partner at this vulnerable early stage by being involved from the outset. In health matters especially, you can influence her and indirectly promote the welfare of that hard-charging, hard-working embryonic child of yours.

Sharing the News

Every newly pregnant couple faces the question of who to tell and when. It's a pleasant sort of dilemma to have. As with so many things during this time, there is no right or wrong approach. There is only the way that you, as a couple, choose to do it and what works for both of you.

Some couples take a cautious approach, preferring to wait to tell people until after three months or so have passed. After this point, the threat of miscarriage drops sharply. The greatest risk of miscarriage is in the first twelve weeks of pregnancy (although it can still occur later). These couples prefer not to tell people the good news and then, if something happens, have to follow this up with bad news. So they wait until they're confident all is right with the baby and things are going swimmingly. Then they reveal the happy news.

Other couples are less cautious. They see no reason to wait, and they eagerly share the good news virtually as soon as they know it themselves. The pleasure in telling people immediately far outweighs the small risk of burdening them with disappointment later. Then there are those who are just not good at keeping a secret. An accidental slip of the tongue arouses a sibling's curiosity, and, before you know it, the whole family knows.

Telling Family and Friends

Some people you are going to want to tell in person, some over the phone and others by e-mail. If your parents live not too far away, for example, it might be a nice gesture to pay them a visit to reveal the news in person. If not, a phone call can do the trick.

One of the advantages of e-mail is that you can tell a large number of people all at once, if you wish. Those on this list may not be super-close friends of yours but acquaintances who are close enough that you still want them to know the news. E-mail can save you lots of time if you're too busy with the excitement of pregnancy to write to or call each person individually.

If you have a regular group of people you play football or pool with or hang out with, tell them in person. Expect some good-natured ribbing about how you are going to be knee-deep in nappies and one of the walking wounded from lack of sleep and all that. This might be a good time to buy a round or two in the pub and experience some old-fashioned male bonding.

Reactions That May Surprise You

With your friends, you probably don't have to worry when you break the news. They are going to offer congratulations, make some jokes and then tell you to shut up and play. But with other people, particularly family members, you may be surprised at their reaction. It may not be what you expected from them.

Although you may be spilling over with excitement, your parents may be instantly shocked into silence or a studied reserve. Remember your surprise when your partner told you she had missed her period? Well, the news may deliver a similar blow to your parents and in-laws. This represents a big event in their lives, too, and it may take them a little time to absorb it all. (Your parents may not feel ready to be grandparents just at this moment!)

This may be true not just for family but friends as well, including your mates. Although they may make jokes, privately one or two may wonder how the baby is going to affect your friendship with them, just as you wonder how it is going to affect your relationship with your partner. One of those guys may have been trying to get pregnant with his wife and so far have been unsuccessful. The fact that you are going to be a father may stir feelings of disappointment, or even jealousy, in him.

Although this book is orientated towards first-time fathers, you may have already had a child. This child may be beside herself with excitement about the prospect of a new brother or sister, but amid these feelings there may also be concern. She may be afraid the baby on the way will replace her in some way and may worry that you will love the new baby more than her.

If the response of your parents or another close family member is somehow less than you expected, don't push it. Allow them the space to have their own personal reaction. They may need time to absorb the implications, just as you did.

Early Workplace Strategies

The fact that you are going to have a baby has an obvious importance in your personal and social life. But there is another important aspect of this news for both men and women: its impact on work. How do you tell your employer? And when is the best time to do that? These are questions every couple must address sooner or later.

This, again, is another issue you two need to discuss as a couple. After the baby comes, one of you certainly needs to have a steady income. In most cases, that will be the man. But your partner may need (or want) to resume her career after the baby is born. So both of you may need to be a little cagey in how you handle the news of your pregnancy at work.

Assessing the Ground

In some companies, you may be able to walk right into your boss's office and blurt out, 'Hey, I'm going to have a baby!' Your boss will stand up, shake your hand and ask you how much time off you would like when the baby is born. Because, your boss will say, a job is only a job. But having a baby? Ah, nothing is more important than that.

If your company is like this (and you're not dreaming), you don't have a thing to worry about. Many companies, however, are not quite so enlightened. Your first task is to assess the ground. Do not blurt anything out just yet. Make sure you are covered first before you make a move.

You will be the best judge of your company's work culture. Is it going to be receptive to the idea of your becoming a parent? Many companies, frankly, are not (though they may say otherwise in statements for public consumption). When you become a parent, you are no longer solely devoted to your job, and your employer may view you differently.

Talk to Colleagues

Talk to a trusted friend at work who is also a father to help you gauge how receptive the management will be. The friend can give you the lowdown on the best way to approach your boss or how to handle the situation with the company in general. He may tell you that any worries are groundless and that you can proceed with confidence. Or he may give you advice on how to avoid some of the pitfalls, if any, he encountered.

Large companies are often committed to family-friendly policies. Similarly, jobs in public-sector organizations often come with clear-cut commitments to family-friendly hours and conditions. In both cases, it should be easy to find out what policies the organization has. But things are often harder in smaller companies. They may profess willingness to support parents' needs but don't actually deliver. You may encounter hostility from managers and staff, too. Sometimes, you can persuade or influence an employer to adopt flexible working hours or other family-friendly policies.

When seeking advice on any pregnancy-related topic, you will also find a natural ally in mothers. Because they have children themselves, they will be supportive of a man who wants to be an involved father. If you work in a department or company with a lot of women, they are likely to be more receptive to your pending fatherhood and the responsibilities it will entail than colleagues in a male-dominated environment.

Telling the Boss

It is generally not a good idea to talk to your boss about your pending fatherhood until you have done some homework about your company policies on paternal leave and similar issues. You also need to have a clear idea of what your plans are. For instance, how much time do you want to take off when the baby comes? You cannot really answer that question until you take a hard look at your financial picture in combination with what your job will allow.

While you may want to immediately tell your parents or close friends that you are about to become a father, it is probably wise to wait at least until three months have elapsed before talking about it at work. This will still give you, and them, plenty of time to plan. Also, if there is a rise or promotion for you in the offing, and you are aware of what's brewing, definitely wait until you get it before you break the news to your boss. You deserve that rise; you will need every penny of it when the baby comes. You do not want to take any chances on preventing it from occurring.

Business Owner or Self-Employed

Many fathers-to-be run their own businesses. They are in the enviable position of not having to ask for time off from a boss; they are the boss and can just take the time. But depending on the size of their business, they may not have another employee who can simply step in for them while they take a week or two off.

Other fathers-to-be are self-employed and work at home. They have no staff at all. When they stop working, their entire business shuts down. With these men, as well as men who are employees in a company, there will be pressure on them to get back to work as soon as possible after the baby is born. These and other work-related pressures and stresses are considered in Chapter 9.

Learning that you are about to become a father can turn your world upside down. There are your own feelings to deal with, not to mention your partner's. You also have to deal with many other people – your families (hers and yours), doctors and medical specialists, to name only a few. Then there are the issues of work and money. Nobody has all the answers in the beginning, but in the months to come you will sort them out.

Chapter 3

Riding the Pregnancy Roller Coaster

Being a father-to-be is like riding a roller coaster. You and your pregnant partner (especially your partner!) go up and down, and down and up, in a crazy, emotion-charged experience. Particularly in the early months, with the onset of morning sickness and the beginning of weight gain, the ride can be bumpy and unpredictable. Here is what to expect as you negotiate the curves.

The Stages of Pregnancy

Every man learns lots of new things in the process of becoming a father, including a few new words to add to his vocabulary. One of those words is 'trimester'. A trimester is one-third of a pregnancy, or roughly three months. Each trimester represents a distinct stage in your child's development, and each carries its own rewards and challenges for both you and your partner.

As unique as every child is, as individual as every woman, the process of having a baby is a fairly patterned process. Although there are endless small variations, the same things basically happen at the same time in every pregnancy. Many people have been down this road before. It is worth having a basic grasp of what happens during each of the three trimesters of pregnancy because this will help you understand not only what you are going through at the moment, but also what lies ahead.

The First Trimester

The first trimester is approximately the first three months of the pregnancy. This is the beginning of the ride. In this period, your partner may still look like she has always looked. Appearances can be deceiving, though. Inside her body, hormones and other chemicals are shooting off like fireworks on Guy Fawkes' Night. Incredible metabolic changes are occurring, although these may not be immediately apparent.

During the first few months, the child inside the womb grows with amazing rapidity. The umbilical cord is as thin as a human hair, yet the baby's tiny brain already has a skull around it. She has a sense of smell, and eyes and ears are formed. The fingers on her hands are segmenting. By the end of the first trimester she can even suck her thumb.

Generally, however, your partner will probably start to act a little differently from normal. Almost certainly she will become very, very tired. The ordinary chores of life – getting up in the morning to go to work, to name a big one – will be harder for her. In the early evening, after a day spent at work, she will probably be crashed out on the sofa. This sudden fatigue she feels is brought on by the overtime her body is putting in on the pregnancy.

The changes you have heard so much about are beginning to occur. You do not have to wait for the baby to arrive to see changes in your partner or your relationship. They happen nearly at once, with the onset of pregnancy in the first trimester.

The Second, or Middle, Trimester

The second trimester is the middle three months of pregnancy, what you might call 'the lull between storms'. Although every woman is different, this is often the rosiest time of the pregnancy for both of you. Morning sickness and the extreme exhaustion have usually passed. She is beginning to show and is proud of it, but the baby is not so big yet that the pregnancy has become a huge burden, weighing her down physically and emotionally. You feel relieved because your partner is acting like herself again.

Many pregnant women report feeling on top of the world during this time, with energy surging through them. This renewed energy may allow the two of you to get reacquainted in the bedroom. The middle trimester is a good time to schedule a romantic weekend getaway or to finally do that one thing you two have always wanted to do as a couple. Pretty soon your partner's nesting instincts will kick in, and after the baby is born it will be a fair bit harder to go out together for a while, so now is the time.

One of the highlights of this period is that you get to feel the baby kick for the first time. Your partner lies on the bed or the sofa, and you put your hand on her abdomen. At first all you can hear is her stomach growling, but you wait... and are still... and wait some more... and then, boom! There it is. At that moment you would not trade your place in life with any man in the world.

The strong movements you feel the baby making at this stage happen because he has well-developed arms and legs. He is working them out. He has periods of activity and longer periods of calm in which he does not move at all. Able to react to sounds outside the womb, he can distinguish the voices of his mother and father by this time.

The Final Trimester

The last trimester is the home straight, the final leg of this marathon. Although each trimester roughly covers the same length of time, this one can feel like the longest of all. Your partner feels as big as a house, and everything she does – sitting, standing up, walking – is a monumental effort for her. Because of this, she is not always in the best of moods. Day by day she becomes more and more eager for the baby to be born, partly so the two of you can meet the newcomer but also so she can have her body to herself again.

The changes, as always, keep coming. Your partner may have left her job because she is simply too tired and uncomfortable to work any more. She may be having what are called Braxton Hicks contractions, a sort of preparatory muscle movement that is readying her body to give birth. The baby, who weighs 2.5–3.5kg (6–8lb) (or more) and is about 51cm (20in) long, sits right on her bladder. This makes her have to pee almost as often as you do when you're drinking beer.

The closer you get to the due date, the more anxious you both become. Your partner visits the midwife or doctor once a week. She may not like to go out in public any more because she's so uncomfortable. The two of you stay in closer touch with each other, just as your family and friends check in more often to see if there's anything they can do. But it's just a waiting game now.

Pregnancy is a minefield for fathers-to-be. Even the most innocuous remark can drive your partner to tears or make her angrier than hell at you. Be careful what you say. When in doubt, bite your tongue and say nothing, and you will be better off in the long run.

Morning Sickness

Morning sickness usually takes place in the first three months of pregnancy. Some lucky women experience it only slightly or not at all, while others get raging cases. Morning sickness is actually a misnomer, because it can occur at any time of day – morning, noon and night.

No one knows exactly what causes it. It may be due to the wild and freaky hormonal changes occurring in a woman's body. It will not hurt the baby; in fact, it may help. Researchers have speculated that morning sickness may be nature's way of protecting the developing foetus from toxins that could harm it. And morning sickness seems to suggest a stable pregnancy and a reduced risk of miscarriage.

Morning sickness feels like a bad, bad hangover. Only it's far worse than a hangover because it lasts for weeks and very little can be done to treat it. A woman in the grip of morning sickness feels like throwing up and sometimes does. She may have heartburn or a sour stomach, and ordinary cooking or food smells may seem ghastly and revolting to her. As a result, she may feel like eating only bland foods or maybe eating nothing at all.

This is a trying time for your partner, but there are some things you may be able to do to help. They include the following:

· Remind her to drink lots of fluids, particularly water, to prevent her from becoming dehydrated.
· Do some of the food shopping and preparation yourself, ensuring she gets the protein-rich, high-carbohydrate diet she needs.
· Stick with plain foods, such as rice or yogurt, and stay away from spicy and fatty dishes that may upset her stomach.
· Get her to try to eat small meals throughout the day, rather than a big meal at a single sitting. This is less likely to cause her problems.
· Tell her you love her and that you appreciate what she is already doing for the family.

Studies show that about 50 per cent of all pregnant women experience morning sickness. Another way of looking at this statistic, however, is that 50 per cent do not. Fortunately, morning sickness usually disappears after the first trimester, although a few women suffer nausea and vomiting throughout their pregnancies.

> If your partner's morning sickness symptoms are extreme and a cause of worry, she should talk to her midwife or doctor. This is a good rule of thumb for any concern that might arise during pregnancy, at any stage. Do not hesitate to seek medical advice.

Cravings

Whenever you see fathers-to-be depicted in films or on television, two things invariably happen. One is that the man faints in the delivery room during childbirth (although this almost never happens in real life). The other thing you see occurs earlier in the pregnancy, when the woman develops some strange food craving and sends the man out in the middle of the night to get it for her.

Cravings are a normal and sometimes fun part of pregnancy. Also normal is the opposite of cravings: food aversion. Just as some pregnant women may develop cravings from time to time for pickles or peanut butter, they may also turn their nose up at food or beverages they formerly loved, such as a morning cup of coffee.

As with morning sickness, there are theories why women's bodies instinctively react in this manner. Those raging hormones, as always, lie at the root of it. But it may be that the reason a woman craves certain foods is that her body needs what those foods are supplying her with. Conversely, she may feel repulsed by certain previously indulged-in items, such as coffee or alcohol, because these are potentially harmful to the baby inside.

So what's a man to do if his pregnant partner develops a sudden taste for gooseberry yogurt at four in the morning? The answer to that one is simple. He throws on his clothes, grabs the car keys, and goes to get it. Your partner will consider you a hero, and the two of you can sit in bed and eat gooseberry yogurt together while watching the sun rise.

Studies show that up to 80 per cent of all women experience food aversions of one kind or another during pregnancy. Cravings are even more common, with nine out of ten women saying they hungered for a certain food. The most popular food craving for pregnant women? Ice cream.

Her Changing Body

If most of the attention during pregnancy seems to be focused on the woman, it is because that is where that attention quite properly belongs. The woman is the lead player, and if you have any doubts about that all you have to do is look at her body, which is beginning to look a little, well, large.

The first, last and foremost rule in dealing with your partner's expanding girth during this time is never – never! – make jokes about her body. If she wants to make jokes about it, fine. If she wants to poke fun at herself, fine. But you? *Never.*

You really do want to boost your partner's spirits. She needs all the support she can get because her body is putting her through the mangle. It seems to be changing on a daily, even hourly basis, in a thousand weird and wacky ways. Here are a few of the things that might well be happening to her:

- Constipation and haemorrhoids
- Tender, sore and enlarged breasts
- Super-sensitive nipples
- Leg and stomach cramps
- Heartburn
- Back pain and sciatica
- Aches and pains of all sorts
- Splotchy, flaky or itchy skin
- Breathlessness
- Headaches and tiredness

Your partner has a new, developing shape that she is still learning to live with. Her centre of balance is shifting, making her clumsier at times. She also may be more forgetful than usual, more distracted and absent-minded. Be gentle and patient. After all, she is building your baby.

Sympathy Pains

Some men experience physical sensations when their partner is pregnant. These are commonly known as 'sympathy pains'. Another term for it is the couvade syndrome. *Couvade* is a French word meaning 'hatch'. Another way to explain this is that the rooster feels a little bit of what the hen is going through.

Physical Signs

The most common of these feelings are stomach pains and discomfort. Many men also say they have food cravings, much like their pregnant partner, and some gain weight. These symptoms tend to crop up early in the pregnancy, in the third month or so, and they vanish just as mysteriously as they arrived after the baby is born.

No one knows exactly why this occurs. These feelings are not purely in a man's head, as some might think. They are actual physical sensations. Some speculate that the couvade is another way in which the man tries to protect his partner. Since there is little he can do to ease her discomfort, his brain tries to take on some of these pains and thus relieve her.

Another theory is that male hormones cause these symptoms. Men have hormones just as women do, just in smaller doses. One recent study suggests that a man's hormones change to correspond with the hormonal changes in his pregnant partner's body. This may explain why men who could not have cared less about children for most of their adult lives begin to show more interest in babies in the last months of their partner's pregnancy.

One out of four fathers-to-be experience gastrointestinal discomfort during their partner's pregnancy. Less common aches and pains are headaches, itching, nose bleeds and toothaches. In some cultures, when a man complains of a toothache, his dentist is taught to ask him if his partner is pregnant.

No Sympathy for Your Sympathy Pains

One thing is certain about your sympathy pains: don't expect much sympathy for them. You may wake up in the morning feeling nauseous, or you may notice that you have put on a few extra kilos around the middle during the pregnancy. But you know, along with everyone else, that this is nothing compared to what your partner is going through.

Some people say that sympathy pains are nothing more than the man's attempt to get people to pay attention to him. The man is jealous, in this view, that all the focus in his relationship has shifted to his partner, and he is feeling left out. He wants people to recognize that he is the father and that he's part of this programme, too. In fact, sympathy pains bring up a larger issue that has nothing to do with the pains themselves and everything to do with a man's role during his partner's pregnancy. Chapter 6 covers some of the myriad worries you may experience.

If you're having sympathy pains, do you talk about them with your partner? Most men might mention them in a casual conversation over the breakfast table or in bed. It's no big thing. Your partner may appreciate the fact that you're suffering a little along with her, and she may see it as another sign that you're fully involved with the pregnancy and coming to grips mentally with this huge event in your lives.

A Volatile Issue: Her Weight

Every man knows how sensitive the issue of weight is to some women. It's like a hair-trigger explosive. Touch it in the wrong way – or even touch it at all – and it is going to explode in your face. Most smart men never venture near it. Those who do, do so only at extreme risk.

When women become pregnant, the issue of weight becomes even more sensitive. Suddenly they can no longer fit into their jeans. In fact, none of their clothes fit. Sometimes even their feet grow in size so their shoes don't fit, either. They look in the mirror and see somebody they hardly recognize.

Some women cannot stand the way they look during pregnancy. It is so contrary to their normal body image that they think they look fat and ugly. The early months may be the hardest for them because they're not really showing and yet they're putting on a lot of weight. People who do not know they're pregnant may just think they're gaining weight, and this adds to their misery. These feelings lighten during the middle trimester, when the pregnant woman clearly begins to show.

Average weight gain during pregnancy is 8–15kg (18–32lb). But it is quite common for women to gain as much as 23kg (50lb), or even more, in the months before giving birth. They will shed most of this weight once the baby is born, although the more weight a woman gains, the harder it will be for her to return to her pre-pregnancy self.

All of this puts the man in a quandary. He wants his partner to gain weight. It is what she is supposed to be doing. Her weight gain means that the baby is growing and getting bigger and stronger, all of which is good. But what should he do, if anything, if his partner keeps getting bigger... and bigger... and bigger?

Take Charge of Healthy Eating

One approach is to take charge of doing the food shopping and meal preparation (if you haven't already), so that you know your partner is getting the right kinds of food. Prepare meals full of green, leafy vegetables bursting with folic acid, protein-rich meat, chicken and fish, and other good things. Without needing to say one word about her weight, you can still be helping her in this regard.

Some pregnant women have a different dilemma: not gaining enough weight. This is nothing to be alarmed about early in the pregnancy, but it should be monitored because it can affect the baby's growth later on. Encouraging your partner to eat several small nutrition-packed meals a day may help her put on the pounds.

Another way to help is with meals outside the home. Does she eat junk food? Do you? Taking a little break from the greasy, high-fat meals at fast-food places is not much of a sacrifice to make.

Be fair. You can't expect her to eat healthy foods while you eat chips and doughnuts in front of her. The same holds true for smoking and drinking: don't smoke in her presence, and lower your alcohol intake so she won't be as tempted.

Be Complimentary

Whatever you think of your partner's growing size, you can be certain that criticizing her isn't a good approach. You would like her to gain enough weight so that she and the baby are healthy, but not so much that she has a hard time losing the weight after she gives birth. This may not seem like a lot to ask, but putting her down or making fun of her will surely not help her. She will only resent you for your lack of sympathy, and it may hurt your relationship.

Here's a better tactic: flood her with kindness. Tell her she looks beautiful, and keep telling her that for the next nine months and beyond, even if you secretly are thinking something else. It will make her feel better, and the burden she's carrying will seem a little lighter.

Get into It!

Women gain weight when they're pregnant, to be sure. That's what they're supposed to do. Instead of experiencing it as a negative, however, try seeing it in a different way. Many women look sexy wearing the extra weight that comes with pregnancy. Think of that famous *Vanity Fair* cover shot of the naked and pregnant Demi Moore. Did you ever see any pictures of Catherine Zeta-Jones decked out in a low-cut evening dress while she was five or six months pregnant?

It is not just Hollywood stars who 'glow' during this time. Pregnancy can add vitality to a woman's appearance and curves to her shape that are a real turn-on.

Women's breasts go through a notable change – they get bigger. Although the woman's nipples may become very sensitive, for men, larger and fuller breasts do not generally pose a problem. Even before the baby comes, some women produce milk from their breasts. The taste of breast milk is sweet, and there is no reason why a man cannot enjoy this taste.

The Emotional Roller Coaster

The physical changes that your partner is experiencing may be accompanied by sudden and abrupt mood swings. One minute she is on a hormone-induced high, feeling free as a bird, as good as she has ever felt in her entire life. Five minutes later, tears are pouring down her face because she cannot fasten the top button on her jeans. A little while after that, she feels irritable or defensive and snaps at you for some remark you made that she perceived to be offensive.

While this may appear to be irrational behaviour – and much of it is – put yourself in her shoes. A tiny, demanding, hungry little human being is growing inside her. In many respects, this foetal beast has taken over her body. If this were happening to you, you probably would not be in the cheeriest of moods, either.

Be Even and Steady

When your loving and long-suffering partner behaves a little crazily, you can respond in kind with craziness of your own. When she takes a dig at you, you can dig back. When she yells at you, you can yell back. To some extent, every man is going to find himself doing exactly that. You are not Gandhi, after all. You have emotions just like she does, and you're entitled to show them.

All couples argue, pregnant or not. There is no way to avoid that. Just realize that your partner's emotional state may be more ragged and unpredictable than normal. Be steady as you go. Being a rock to her emotional waves will help in the long run.

Hold Her Hand

One thing you should realize is that the changing nature of your partner's moods may upset her, too. Her body, she has found, is no longer completely under her control. And now her emotions are going crazy on her as well. It may be scary to her and make her think that her entire life is out of balance.

If pregnancy is like a roller-coaster ride, what would you do to comfort your partner if she felt genuinely scared on an actual roller-coaster ride?

What if she began to cry uncontrollably or scream because she feared that the car you were riding in was going to topple over or break? You almost certainly would reach over and hold her hand to reassure her. This is also something you can do for your partner when she is upset or anxious or fearful about her pregnancy. Hold your partner's hand. Caress her hand or forehead. Put your arm around her and embrace her. Rub her feet. Cuddle her in a non-sexual way in bed. Through all these ways and more you can show your partner that you care about her and understand what's she going through.

Another reason why many pregnant women feel miserable is the clothes they must wear. Nice-looking maternity clothes are expensive. Some mothers-to-be only have a couple of outfits that they feel comfortable and look good in, and consequently they wear them to death. Kind words go a long way.

Remember, This Too Shall Pass

The nine to ten months of pregnancy may feel like an eternity at times, but they actually pass fairly quickly, especially when you consider the years and years you are going to spend bringing up your child. It is good to remember throughout pregnancy – and, for that matter, when you're a parent – that this too shall pass. Nothing lasts forever.

Your partner's morning sickness is going to pass. She is going to move on from the first trimester of pregnancy into the middle and later stages. She is going to gain weight, and after the baby comes, she will lose weight. Once the baby arrives, the concerns she had while she was pregnant will be replaced by other concerns that have to do with bringing up a child – concerns that you, as the child's father, will certainly share.

All this is the way it is supposed to be, and is the way it has always been. It is impossible to change any of it, and why would you want to? This may sound trite, but it is true. While you are on this extraordinary journey, try to enjoy each moment as much as possible.

Look at how much you've learned about pregnancy already – the stages that are involved, how quickly (and amazingly) your baby is developing, your partner's changing body and how this can affect her moods. And the great thing is that the more knowledge you have, the less anxious you feel, and the more enjoyable the whole experience becomes. This rule also applies to the process of learning how to be a labour partner and the medical aspects of the pregnancy.

Chapter 4

Doctors and Medical Tests

Having a baby is a physical and emotional experience. It is also a medical one. Midwives, doctors and specialists will help you and your partner deliver your baby. Here are some tips on how to deal with what can be an intimidating world for men.

What's Involved?

Antenatal medicine today is nothing like it was when you were born. It is more technologically advanced (some might say technologically intrusive) than ever. All of these advancements have one goal: a safe and healthy outcome for mother and baby.

Even if you and your partner choose to have the baby at home, instead of in hospital, you will still benefit from this technology as well as the advice and counsel of trained doctors and midwives. Your partner will see a doctor or midwife on a regular basis. During each visit, her urine will be drawn and tested, and her blood may be too, to make sure that the baby's development is proceeding as it should. Your partner (and you, if you go) will have many questions to ask the midwife or doctor.

Ultrasound scans have become a routine part of antenatal medical technology. They are usually performed when a woman first attends the antenatal clinic (at around 10–12 weeks) and at 18–21 weeks of pregnancy. The ultrasound is an exciting event for a couple because it affords you the first chance to see your child and even get a picture of him – your first baby picture.

Medical science is not foolproof, and the act of having a baby still involves a degree of risk for both the mother and the child. Luck and mystery also stick their fingers into the pie. But both mothers- and fathers-to-be can feel a measure of confidence about this new world they're entering because the people in it are highly trained, motivated and experienced professionals whose goal is the same as yours: healthy baby, healthy mother.

The Obstetrician

Next to you and the baby, your partner's obstetrician is the most important person in her life. Family doctors also provide antenatal care. No matter what his or her exact title is, the obstetrician is the person who oversees and coordinates your partner's care.

However, this doctor may not actually deliver your baby. The consultants at your hospital may work on a rotating basis, which means that if your partner's doctor is on duty the night you come in to have your baby, she will be the attending physician. If not, you will get the physician who happens to be on duty that night. If you have gone the private route, the doctor your partner has seen throughout the pregnancy does indeed commit to seeing her all the way through to birth.

The doctor can answer medical questions about pregnancy. And if she does not have the answer to a given question, she can refer you to a specialist who will have the answers you're looking for. But a good doctor has more than just medical skills and know-how. She also functions as a reassuring figure to the nervous mother-to-be, who counts on her as the person who has been down this road many times before and can show her the way.

Your Relationship with Her Doctor

In the not-so-distant past, fathers were seen as unwelcome intruders in a hospital or doctor's surgery. While the attitudes of the medical profession have changed considerably, you may still feel somewhat in the way. You may be treated with coolness, patronized or not taken seriously. When speaking, the doctor may look only at your partner, not at you, even if you were the one who asked the question.

Nowadays, thankfully, few medical professionals act like this. Most see the father as a truly important person, not just someone who gets in the way. They talk to both the man and the woman, answer their questions directly, and treat them as equals who are sharing this adventure together.

Don't act like a potted plant if the doctor treats you coolly or ignores you. Speak up, and ask questions. Make direct eye contact with him. Appear interested and involved. If necessary, tell him directly that you wish to be included.

Being There

Given that many fathers-to-be feel like a spare part when they visit the doctor with their pregnant partners, it is understandable that some choose not to go at all. The partners of these men go there on their own, and the man finds out what he needs to know when the woman gets home. In addition, he may be at work and unable to take the time off.

Even the most involved father-to-be need not attend every antenatal check-up. But every man should go to at least one early in the pregnancy (in addition to the ultrasound). That gives you a chance to meet your partner's doctor or midwife, and to ask questions and get answers directly from a medical expert.

Of course, your partner may need you to go to more than just one or two visits, at which point you are going to have to rearrange your diary and be there. You will certainly want to be on hand for the ultrasound scans and the amniocentesis, if one is called for. At various times during the pregnancy, particularly in the beginning and then later on, as you head down the home straight to the finishing line, she may need you to do nothing more than hold her hand and reassure her. Her doctor may consider you irrelevant, but almost certainly your partner does not see you that way.

Antenatal Doctor Visits

Usually, a pregnant woman pays one or two visits to the midwife or doctor in her first trimester. In the middle trimester, the frequency of her visits increases to about once every six weeks. Entering the final trimester, trips to the doctor become fortnightly affairs until, at about the 36-week mark, she may see the doctor as often as once a week. Depending on your partner's medical history and her specific health issues, a doctor may want to see her more often.

One of the best antenatal visits for dads occurs at about 12 weeks, when you hear the baby's heartbeat for the first time. The doctor lubricates your partner's abdomen with some slippery gel, then runs a handheld ultrasound instrument – known as an ultrasound Doppler – over the lubricated area. The Doppler picks up and amplifies the sound coming from inside the womb. The sound of your child's beating heart is sure to bring a smile.

Hearing the heartbeat is another of those signposts along the pregnancy road that is particularly meaningful to Dad. The idea of having a baby is still pretty abstract to him up to this point. But hearing that little thumper makes it a lot more real. The realization steadily dawns that an actual, honest-to-goodness human being is inside there.

After three months, the baby is 27–32mm (1¹⁄₈–1¹⁄₄in) long, about twice the size of your thumbnail. Her heart, which has been beating for a while, is now strong enough that instruments can pick up the sound. While the foetal heart pumps only one-fifth of the blood of an adult heart, it has already developed valves and four chambers.

Monitoring Progress

A woman undergoes a battery of tests throughout her pregnancy. She is poked at and pricked with needles. Every time she walks into a doctor's surgery, she is asked for a urine sample and has to pee in a cup. Similarly, her weight may be checked rigorously and her blood pressure may be monitored. You may (or may not) be intimidated when you see your partner's doctors and midwives, but by the time her pregnancy is over, they will feel like old friends to her.

The tests performed on your partner are designed to monitor her health, the condition of the developing foetus, and the possible development of any birth defects.

Here are several of the more common tests that are customarily administered at the first antenatal appointment or booking visit, at about 12 weeks:

- Urine tests measure sugar or glucose levels, protein and bacteria.
- Blood tests check for iron deficiency (anaemia) and blood type.
- Blood screens gauge immunity to rubella and other diseases, and check for any signs of syphilis, hepatitis B and, if you agree, HIV and sickle cell anaemia.
- Triple screen or expanded alpha-foetoprotein blood test checks for possible birth defects (second trimester).

- Glucose screening tests for gestational diabetes (also usually in second trimester).
- Some maternity units also offer a nuchal ultrasound scan at around 11–14 weeks, which is a screening test for Down's syndrome. This can't tell you for certain whether or not your baby is affected – it only suggests what the risk is.
- If screening tests suggest that your baby is at risk of having spina bifida or Down's syndrome, you may choose to have a diagnostic test, which can tell you for certain. These include amniocentesis and chorionic villus sampling (see page 50).

Medical test results are often loaded down with numbers that mean something to doctors but almost nothing to lay people. You and your partner may have questions after these tests are done, especially if the results are not what you expected. This is definitely a good time to go with your partner to her doctor. Writing down your questions before the appointment will help you remember everything you want to ask in the sometimes rushed, high-pressure environment of a clinic.

Ultrasound Scans

Going to the ultrasound scan is one of the early highlights of pregnancy. It's the first time you will see your baby (well, sort of). Two ultrasounds may be conducted early in pregnancy – the first (dating) scan is usually done at around 10–12 weeks, and the second between eighteen and twenty-one weeks. Both visits are a wake-up call that you absolutely must not miss.

Ultrasound technology, known as sonography, represents a major step forward in obstetrics. It uses sound waves that are inaudible to the human ear to create a visual image of the baby's environment inside the womb – not a television-quality image, mind you, but an image nonetheless. An ultrasound or sonogram is not an X-ray and is regarded as completely safe. Even so, it is done only when medically necessary.

Medical tests are not 100 per cent accurate. A false negative may indicate that something is all right when it isn't. These instances are rare, though. More common are false positives, in which the test indicates there is a problem when actually everything is fine. Discuss test results with your doctor or midwife, and get a second opinion if necessary.

What Ultrasound Does

An ultrasound scan provides lots of vital information. It can provide accurate information about how far along your partner is in the pregnancy and nail down the baby's due date. It can help doctors look for abnormalities in the foetus and note how it is developing. The ultrasound also provides a wealth of technical information, such as the amount of amniotic fluid in the amniotic sac, what kind of shape the placenta is in (and where it is) and other hard facts.

An ultrasound scan may carry a surprise or two as well. You may learn that you have not one but two foetuses swimming around in there. A sonographer may also be able to ascertain whether your child is a boy or a girl, if you wish to know.

What You Can Expect

Because an ultrasound scan is such a big moment in the life of pregnant couples, sonographers are quite comfortable with having men around. In some ways an ultrasound resembles a good television show. Both you and your partner will have your eyes glued to the monitor, trying to detect every possible detail about your child. Meanwhile, the sonographer serves as your host and guide, telling you exactly what you are looking at as she records the information she needs to know.

Your partner lies on her back on a table, exposing her stomach. The sonographer rubs some lubricating gel on her skin and places a device on her abdomen that directs sound waves at her uterus and foetus. The echoes created by these sound waves produce the visual images you see on the monitor.

But don't expect to see too much. Reading the monitor is like trying to read a traffic sign fifty metres away in the middle of a blizzard. Still, it is an exciting experience, like being given the chance to peer into this secret world. With the sonographer's assistance, you will be able to pinpoint features on your child – his hands and arms, his legs and feet, his head and his beating heart. When the 10–15-minute visit is over, you get a picture of your baby that you can show your friends and family and tape to the front of your refrigerator at home.

Boy or Girl?

In addition to the fact that the ultrasound gives couples the chance to see their baby for the first time, it is an important event in the life of a couple for another reason. This is often when you learn your child's gender. Although parents-to-be can learn whether the baby is a boy or a girl at the first ultrasound (around the 10–12-week mark), this revelation generally occurs during the second visit, at roughly the 20-week point in the pregnancy. The foetus is larger, and his or her gender is easier to identify (although it is not always possible to tell for certain).

Although the technology continues to improve and the pictures that they rely on are becoming ever clearer, sonographers have been known to make mistakes in guessing a child's gender. Because their determinations are based on visual evidence, they are not 100 per cent accurate. The great majority of the time, though, sonographers are accurate.

You and your partner must decide. Do you want to know the gender? As with so many things having to do with pregnancy, there is no right or wrong decision, and nobody else can make it. Whatever works for the two of you – that is the right decision.

Some couples prefer not to know. They enjoy the guessing game and the suspense leading up to the big moment when the baby is finally born. If you do not want to know your child's gender, make sure to tell your doctor and the people at the ultrasound scan. You do not want them to spill the beans accidentally.

Other couples choose not to wait until after the baby is born to find out; they want to know as soon as they can. There are some practical advantages to this approach. Knowing the baby's gender may make it easier to decide on nursery decorations or what kind of clothes to buy. In addition, there is only one name to choose.

The Moment You Learn the News

Just as when your partner told you she was pregnant you were in a reactive position, you will be reacting again when you learn the gender of your child. Unlike when you heard about the pregnancy for the first time, however, this information is not news that your partner necessarily has first. She does not know the child's gender; she is as out of the picture as you are. The one with the information is the sonographer. This is the person who will tell you whether you have a boy or girl.

Your partner is lying on her back with her head turned to look at the monitor while the sonographer moves the ultrasound device around her belly. This is not a comfortable position for her, nor a relaxed moment. She is happy, excited, anxious, nervous, fearful and curious – all at the same time.

One reason for her anxiety is you. Whether she says so or not, she is searching your face for clues about how you feel. The sonographer has just told you the news – boy or girl – and your partner, in her discomfort on the table, is looking to you for your reaction. Once again, what you do and say in this moment matters – a lot.

The Choices You Make

Each man will have his own reaction when he learns the gender of his child. Although the geneticists point out that the creation of a boy or a girl is a random act, merely a matter of the victorious sperm's chromosomal make-up, everyone knows that it is much more than that. It is big, and the issues it engenders are complex.

Many fathers-to-be want to have a son. Although they may not be willing to admit it, they feel that having a son signifies virility. They may believe that people will consider them more masculine if they have a son. They may also feel as if they are likely to have more in common with a boy than a girl.

A child's gender is determined at the instant of creation. Human beings have 23 pairs, or sets, of chromosomes. The 23rd set is known as the sex chromosomes. In females, the sex chromosomes are XX, while in males, they are XY. The unfertilized egg carries only X, or female, chromosomes. If the egg is fertilized by a sperm carrying only the X chromosome, the foetus gets an X from the sperm and an X from the egg – making it XX, or female. If the sperm that fertilizes the egg carries Y, the foetus gets the Y from the sperm and an X from the egg – making it XY, or male.

A smaller proportion of men want a daughter. For one reason or another, they're not sure about boys. For them, a boy might represent a potential threat to their status. With Mum and daughter around, they will be the man in the family, and they like that.

Sonographers report that some men sulk after hearing the news of their child's gender. They suddenly lose interest in what is going on. Their attention strays. They pick up a magazine and begin leafing through the pages or even stand up and leave the room.

If your first reaction is disappointment or ambivalence, remember that love is not static. Your feelings are only beginning, and they will grow and deepen over time – no matter what the gender of your child. In addition, remember that woman lying on the table gazing up at you for your reaction? She needs you – it's as simple as that. Reach over and hold her hand.

Surprise! It's Twins!

The other big piece of news you could learn at the ultrasound is that you're having twins. Based on some of the symptoms your partner has been experiencing, her doctor may have suspected as much. The sonogram may have been requested to confirm a preliminary diagnosis. An ultrasound scan will be able to detect the presence of twins in almost every case.

Carrying twins (or triplets or other multiples) is considered a 'high-risk' pregnancy. This term is nothing to get frightened about – women deliver twins safely all the time. In fact, nearly one out of every 41 couples has twins these days. But the medical issues involved in carrying and delivering twins are more complicated than if you're just having one. You and your partner need to have a sit-down talk with your obstetrician to get straight on how you're going to proceed from here.

As the prospective father of twins, you may have greater responsibilities during your partner's pregnancy than other fathers-to-be. Your partner is, in effect, doing double duty, and you may need to pitch in extra to help her out. Here are some things to be aware of:

· Your partner will need to see the doctor more often, which may require you to go to more visits.
· Because low birth weight can be a problem for some twins, her diet is crucial, which may mean you need to shop for food and cook more.
· She will need a lot of rest, so you'll need to pitch in with more of the housework and other duties.
· Her doctor may recommend that she stop working after only six or seven months, which means that you may need to get your financial house in order sooner than other fathers-to-be.
· Because twins frequently arrive weeks earlier than a standard pregnancy, you and your partner should take childbirth classes in the second trimester and make sure you know the signs of early labour.

The parents of twins sometimes have an intense emotional reaction when they learn the news that they are going to have two babies at once. Many are in shock at first. Slowly this shock may turn into worry or disappointment or even fear. Such feelings are normal, and there is no reason to feel guilty about having them.

If you're worried about having twins on the way, talk to your partner about it. You may also be able to confide in a close friend, a family member or another parent who has already gone through it. The main thing is to be sure you give yourself some time to adjust to the news.

Amniocentesis and CVS

The ultrasound is a tool used by doctors to diagnose the condition of the growing child and look for possible birth defects or other problems. Two other commonly used diagnostic tools are chorionic villus sampling, or CVS, and amniocentesis, although many couples never have either of these tests done. Both tests have a small degree of risk attached, and they are only performed when there are clear benefits to be gained.

CVS is recommended when there is a family history of genetic disease or if it has been established that the parents are carriers of a disease. It is done early in the pregnancy, between 10 and 12 weeks. CVS is a surgical procedure, usually performed in a hospital, in which a small sample is taken from the placenta. Chromosomal analysis of this tissue can detect the presence of Down's syndrome, many forms of cystic fibrosis and other genetic disorders.

Amniocentesis or CVS is recommended for pregnant women aged 35 or older – what the medical profession describes as 'advanced maternal age'. Younger women normally do not need to consider this procedure. Even some women aged 35 and older choose not to have it. It is an optional procedure that couples may decline if they wish.

The primary purpose of an 'amnio', as it is called, is to see if the foetus has Down's syndrome, which occurs most frequently in women of 'advanced maternal age'. But it is also used to test for spina bifida and other chromosomal defects as well. An amnio usually takes place in hospital in the second trimester, between the 16th and 18th weeks. The procedure is often done in conjunction with the second ultrasound visit.

In an amniocentesis, your partner lies on her back just as she did during the ultrasound. Using the sonograph as a guide, a physician inserts a hollow needle into her stomach though the wall of the abdomen. Amniotic fluids are withdrawn from the womb through the needle. It takes one to two weeks to get the results of the laboratory analysis of the baby's cells in the fluid. Amnio will also establish for certain the gender of your child (though it is never done just for this purpose).

The advantage of CVS over amniocentesis is that it is performed much earlier. However, while it can detect chromosomal abnormalities, it does not detect spina bifida. Many hospitals offer CVS and in recent years it has become a popular alternative to amniocentesis.

One reason why both CVS and amniocentesis are serious medical procedures is that each carries a small risk of miscarriage (about 1 in 200). You and your partner must weigh this risk against the benefits to be obtained from either procedure. Your doctor can help lay out the clinical facts, but ultimately, like so many other issues having to do with your child, the two of you will make a decision based on your values and what you feel is the right thing to do.

Your partner will feel physically and emotionally drained after a CVS or amniocentesis test. She should be driven home or go in a taxi and spend the rest of the day relaxing quietly. Make sure she avoids vigorous exercise – and do not have sex for three days. Abdominal cramps and a slight loss of blood from the vagina in the first 24 hours after the test are normal but if your partner notices clear fluid leaking from her vagina, she should contact her doctor or midwife straight away.

Threat of Miscarriage

Miscarriage (sometimes known as 'spontaneous abortion') is the loss of a child during pregnancy. It can occur for a variety of reasons, some known and some unknown. When it occurs, it can be an emotionally devastating event for both parents.

The risk of miscarriage is highest in the first trimester. Most miscarriages occur within the first 12 weeks of pregnancy, although they can and do occur later on. It is thought that miscarriages occur in 10 per cent of all reported pregnancies. After suffering a miscarriage, however, nearly nine in ten women have a healthy pregnancy the next time.

Living with the Threat

Because of worry about the possibility of miscarriage, many couples do not immediately tell other people that they are pregnant. They wait until three months have passed, the period considered most likely for a miscarriage, before breaking the news. Some older couples wait even longer, until after reviewing the amniocentesis results at roughly the 20-week mark. When that goes well and everything is fine with the baby, they let their families and friends in on the secret.

Your partner may feel the threat of miscarriage more acutely than you do. On top of the many physical discomforts she experiences early in pregnancy, she may worry that she will do something that will cause her to lose her child. This is another thing to keep in mind as her emotions swing up and down during this vulnerable time.

There are several warning signs of potential miscarriage, such as spotting or bleeding and severe abdominal cramps. If your partner reports these symptoms, you should act immediately. Call your doctor or medical midwife immediately; they will advise you what to do next.

Sex and Miscarriage

Early miscarriage remains shrouded in mystery. No one knows exactly what causes it in many cases. A healthy woman who is doing everything right can still lose a child. One thing a man may wonder about is sexual intercourse. Can it harm the baby or cause a miscarriage? In a normal pregnancy, the answer is no. But talk to the doctor if your partner's pregnancy is considered high-risk or if she has a history of miscarriage.

Another thing a man thinks about is how much weight his partner can safely pick up and carry when she's pregnant. She can continue to do normal household activities, such as carrying light bags of shopping and carefully picking up young children. These will not normally cause harm. Moving large furniture or heavy objects, however, should be your job.

The Emotional Toll

Losing a child, even a child who is still in the womb, can take a heavy emotional toll on the parents. It seems so unfair, so random. So many other couples have babies. Why can't we have one? Why us?

A woman may blame herself. She may feel intense guilt over the loss, as if she were responsible for it. She may become depressed. You may also experience similar feelings of sadness and disappointment.

Not every miscarriage, though, is by definition an awful event. Some mothers express a sense of relief because they inwardly felt something was wrong with the pregnancy. Nature took its course, for whatever reason, and they are willing to accept it and go on.

Trying Again

It is probably going to take some time before you are both ready to move on and try again. You will certainly need to do plenty of talking. And it may be valuable for both you and your partner to talk to other parents who have experienced a loss of this kind. Your local hospital may know of or run a support group for parents who have suffered a miscarriage.

Go with your partner to at least one or two of these sessions. You may be surprised at who you meet there. You may find other men there who have lost children and are grieving about it. They will tell the story of what happened to them, and then you can tell your story. Through this process of talking, you will probably discover feelings of grief and hurt that you did not know were there.

Many, many couples become pregnant again and have a child after a miscarriage. If there were known medical reasons that caused the event, however, you may need to resolve those issues before trying again. Some doctors recommend waiting six months or so for your partner's body to recover. No one but you and your partner, however, can decide when you are ready to give it another go. Before moving on, it is worthwhile to take some time to absorb the loss and let the wounds heal.

Chapter 5

Your Suddenly Expanding Family

When you learn your partner is pregnant, you obviously expect to welcome, at some point, a new person into your family. But a baby widens your social circle beyond just you and your partner. Suddenly a whole load of people – parents, parents-in-law, aunts- and uncles-to-be, other relatives, your partner's close friends – become an intimate part of your life.

Your Shifting Social World

Having a child is one of the greatest things that can happen to a man, but it still causes worry. One of the potential trouble spots (or so a father-to-be thinks) is in the social arena, particularly as it relates to his partner. Many men consider that their partner is their best friend. She provides their deepest emotional support. She is the social leader of the family, inviting friends over for dinner and arranging get-togethers. How will that change when the baby comes?

Your Partner

Almost certainly, if your partner is pregnant, you have already noticed subtle shifts beginning to take place in your social world. Some of these shifts may not be subtle at all. Your partner may be utterly exhausted when she gets home from work and fast asleep on the sofa by eight o'clock. On the weekends she may be too tired to go out.

With your partner crashing out early most nights, you have to do more chores around the house, which puts a dent in your free time. Not only that, you're more tired. When you finally do get a chance to go out with your friends, you feel guilty because you're out enjoying yourself while your partner is stuck at home. So maybe you cut the night short, making your friends think you're already turning into a bore even before the baby is born.

It is important to realize that your social life does not end when you have a baby. All it does is change. In many ways, it changes for the better. Still, these changes can be unsettling at first.

If you're feeling cut off from your partner's whirl in the pregnancy social circle, there is a simple solution — join it. Accompany her on her visits to the clinic. Join in the childbirth classes. Talk to her about baby names. Spend an afternoon with her shopping for baby clothes or gear. It won't kill you, and you may even enjoy it.

Your Friends

One of the things that happens when your partner becomes pregnant is that your social life becomes far less spontaneous. In the old days, your friends might have called you at the last minute to go to the cinema or hear some live music. If it sounded like fun, you went along without thinking twice about it. That is much less likely to happen nowadays.

Or maybe you're worried about your male friends. Many of them may be in their 20s or 30s. They may be single and childless. When baby arrives and you're knee-deep in nappies, how will they react?

For obvious reasons, your childless friends are going to have a harder time adjusting to your new reality. They're still able to go to the pub or out to dinner whenever they feel like it. After you turn down their invitations to go out a couple of times in a row, they may mentally stick you in the 'Married with Children' column and stop calling altogether. And you may find it harder to find the time to call them.

It is inevitable that you will see less and less of your friends who don't have children than you did before. What happens is that they will be slowly replaced with a different sort of animal – couples with small children like your own. Along with your expanding extended family, these people steadily become fixtures in your new social world.

Her Family

One of the biggest changes that occurs in your social world when your partner becomes pregnant is that her relatives and friends become more involved in your family life than ever before. Similarly, you become more involved with them. Because they are ringing the house more often, you talk on the phone more with them. Because they are dropping by to see your partner more often, you are likely to have more occasions to see them as well.

No matter how many years you have been married or in a relationship with the mother-to-be, or how well you think you know your in-laws, with a baby on the way you are going to have an opportunity get to know them much, much better.

Your Mother-in-Law

Like the father who faints on the delivery room floor during childbirth, on TV and in film comedies the mother-in-law is often depicted as a loud, pushy, overbearing, domineering woman who bosses everyone around, including the mother- and father-to-be. Like the fainting dad, this caricature usually bears little relation to reality.

Whatever your mother-in-law's personality, she does have one thing that you and your partner do not yet possess: actual, real-life baby experience. She did it. In fact, she bore and brought up the girl who grew up to be the woman you fell in love with and chose to make the mother of your child, so listen to what your mother-in-law says with an open mind.

Make no mistake. Your mother-in-law – along with your own mother and probably every other person you know in the world – will be giving you advice. You will receive advice on everything under the sun having to do with babies because, well, that is what happens when you are about to become a parent. People give you advice, whether you ask for it or not.

According to a recent study carried out for the Department of Education and Science, 58 per cent of households had relied on a grandparent for childcare in the last year. If your partner plans to go back to work, this option is worth considering. First, you can generally trust your relatives to have your baby's best interests at heart; second, if they have a similar childrearing philosophy to you, it's great; and third, this arrangement will probably give your baby more love and security than any other.

Depending on their personalities, your mother-in-law and mother may be leaders in the advice sweepstakes. Some of what they say will be hard to hear. Some of it will sound like criticism. But every now and then, their words hit the bull's-eye and you will be deeply grateful for their advice.

Your Father-in-Law

In television sitcoms and films, the father-in-law is also a comic figure like the mother-in-law. But unlike her, the father-in-law is usually a quiet type, a man who has become used to being pushed around over the years and has learned to live with it. Again, this caricature may or may not have anything to do with your reality. Still, that doesn't mean that fathers-in-law won't offer advice. They know a thing or two about being a parent, and they will no doubt share it with you at some point. Don't disregard their perspectives. One thing they may confess to you is how lucky they think you are to participate in your child's birth, something that men did not do in their time.

What if I don't get along with an in-law?
Don't fret. The pregnancy has improved your position in the family hierarchy. The in-laws will want to have a relationship with their grandchild, and they will want to be on good terms with the baby's father, too.

Other Family Members and Friends

All the members of your partner's family and her friends are excited about the coming arrival. This is why they are becoming a bigger presence in her life and, indirectly, in yours too. But excitement is not the only reason for this flutter of activity. They are also experiencing a variety of emotions, such as these:

·   They are worried about the physical health and well-being of your partner.
·   They know that things can sometimes go wrong, and they want nothing bad to happen to her.
·   They want the baby to be healthy and normal.
·   They are concerned about you, too, because they know this is putting pressure on you as well.
·   They wonder how your family is doing and how they are handling the news.
·   They are eager to do something and want to know whether they can help in any capacity.

What is interesting to realize is that your partner's family and friends are thinking and feeling much the same things you are. You all have a lot in common, in other words. If you were not close before, you and her family are being drawn together, even if it is just a little bit. This is another of the shifts that a baby can cause, to bring you closer to your extended family.

Your Family

The imminent arrival of a newborn can bring families and friends together. But it can also cause friction sometimes. If one family – say, your partner's – moves strongly into the picture, it may cause your family to withdraw or become resentful in some way of all the time the other side is spending with the baby.

This is how it works when you have a baby. Before, it was just you and your partner. Now that you are about to become a threesome, your extended family is likely to become much more involved in your lives. Usually this is a good thing, but sometimes there are issues to deal with because of it.

Your Mother

When a woman becomes pregnant, she almost inevitably draws closer to her mother, who, having gone through all of this before, is a reassuring and comforting figure. Even if the two live 3,000 miles apart, they find ways to connect. Maybe they e-mail, or maybe they choose to talk more on the phone. The mother comes to visit, and the daughter goes to visit, too. If her mother lives close by, the two often become like girlfriends, shopping for baby clothes, checking out baby gear and so forth.

It is simply not the same experience for fathers-to-be and their mothers. In fact, what may happen is that the man becomes closer to his partner's mother because he starts seeing her more frequently than he did before. And this leaves his own mother feeling left out.

Again, this scenario may never happen. Because you are going to be a parent, and because you will have a little better understanding of what your mother went through all those years bringing you up, the two of you may grow closer as well during this time. In any case, it pays to be sensitive to the feelings of your mother, too.

 If you sense that your mother is feeling left out of what is going on, call her with an update on the pregnancy. Better still, meet her and your father for lunch or invite them to stay. Let them know that you want them to be involved in their grandchild's life.

Your Father

Your father is going through his own set of changes, which may be similar to what your mother is experiencing. Not every man or woman who becomes a parent is initially thrilled with the idea. The same is true for grandparents. While they may love their grandchildren, some older people hate the idea of being called 'Granny' or 'Grandpa' because it makes them feel ancient. For this reason and others, some grandparents never really develop much of a relationship with their grandchildren.

Not your father, though. He is tickled pink about becoming a grandfather. In fact, he has been pestering you for years about having children and still wonders why it took you so long to get around to it. He can't wait to take the baby to the park and buy her a scooter when she's old enough and fly kites with her. But change nappies? No, no, no, that's your job, son.

Accepting Help

Because having a baby represents such a huge transition in your life – not only for you and your partner, but your family and friends as well – you may feel a certain amount of stress as a result of this. But this stress need not be overwhelming. Your family and friends are actually a tremendous resource. Once you come to accept this (and it does take time), your relations with them may go more smoothly.

Your family and in-laws may be completely, massively barking mad. They may be bossy and intrusive at times. They may be a royal pain in the you-know-what. But most definitely they want to be useful and help you. Here are some jobs they can do:

· Go with your partner to the antenatal clinic if you can't make it.
· Be on the lookout for good deals on baby gear and clothes.
· Help you paint the nursery or build the crib.
· Help you financially by hiring a once-a-month cleaning service or nappy service.
· Assist you with the birth (talk to your partner before you make this offer to anyone).
· Help you make phone calls to people after the baby is born.
· Cook meals ahead of time for you to stick in the freezer and defrost and eat after the baby comes.

Because they are eager to help, your family and friends will generally be happy and grateful to do the things you ask. As you will find as you get closer and closer to the due date, it is hard to sit around and wait. Having things to do will make the waiting easier for everyone.

Feelings of Isolation

It is possible, of course, that in the midst of all this family togetherness, with all these giddy feelings of expectation for the baby on the way, someone may feel left out. That someone may be you. You may feel like an outsider even in the middle of a joyous family celebration.

Things have changed in your life, and you're not entirely thrilled about it. You used to hang out with your mates after work; well, that isn't happening so much any more. And when the baby arrives, you get this uneasy feeling in the pit of your stomach that this sort of thing isn't going to happen ever again.

Even as some of your friends are steadily receding from your social circle, your extended family – hers and yours – is coming forwards in a big way to fill the gap. Frankly, you may not be too thrilled about that one, either. It seems like you've seen your mother-in-law and some of your partner's friends more in the past six months than you ever did before.

And what do they all talk about? Baby, baby, baby.

Maybe you realize intellectually that you're not irrelevant – that your partner does, in fact, need you, and your baby, when he comes, will need you too. And you recognize that it is right and good that all these other people are excited about the baby. You're excited too – you really are. Still, there is no denying it. At times you feel isolated and alone, merely a spectator of this parade passing by.

Coping Strategies

There is a lot of stress that comes with being an expectant father. You have a lot to think about, a lot to plan and a lot of changes to absorb in what seems like an awfully short time. New demands are coming at you from your partner and family. Meanwhile, you may already be working harder to make more money for when the baby arrives.

Men and women tend to cope with stress in different ways. Women generally eat more and exercise less. Men, on the other hand, often drink more and watch more television. Many health problems are related to stress. They can be helped by eating better, taking time off work and getting regular exercise.

Some of these pressures are real and need to be addressed, such as money. But some of the stresses you're feeling may be self-induced. Since you've never had a baby before, you don't know what to expect. This may make you put more pressure on yourself than you really need to.

Exercise Is the Way

Exercise is a proven method of controlling stress. The reason for this is simple – it works. You're going to feel better about yourself and your situation after you spend an hour in the gym, or you go for a jog or a 10-mile bike ride. Whatever you do to get your head on straight, do it. And keep doing it as regularly as you can.

Pregnancy changes your world, but it is nothing like what will happen after the baby arrives. Then you have very little time to do anything, including exercise. Now you still have a great deal of freedom and free time, comparatively speaking, so take advantage of both while you can.

Go Out with Your Mates

OK, so maybe it's not exactly the way it used to be with you and your friends. But you're a man. As such, you still have to blow off a little steam now and then. Even Mr Dependability gets to take a night off.

And that is what you need to do – take a night off. Or maybe it's time to really get away from everything. Take a day or two off work and go walking with a group of mates for a long weekend.

Your partner will understand. She may even encourage you to go. Just because she is tired and feels like staying at home doesn't mean you always have to do the same.

Be aware of the due date before you schedule your getaway. This is also true for travel at work. You need to stay close to the home front for at least a month before the baby is due. Neither you nor your partner will be comfortable with you away too near the time that the baby is due.

Keep Things Normal

Another way to manage stress is to take the opposite approach. Instead of going on a big getaway, keep things as normal as possible. Stick to your regular routine, as long as your routine works for you.

Although the regular workday routine can sometimes be a grind, it can also provide a great deal of comfort for the father-to-be. Getting on the bus or train, putting in your eight hours, doing your job, seeing the people you see there, going home at the end of the day – this is a solid structure in a constantly shifting world. And with a baby on the way, you may indeed feel like your world is shifting daily.

Think Positive

Your family, which once consisted almost exclusively of you and your partner, is now a more crowded place. Like it or not, so many more people are part of it – including this child, whom you've never met and who's still being formed, but who is already making her presence felt.

What you can do is keep a positive attitude. These changes, you will find, are not so bad after all. Everything is going to be just fine.

Part of what it means to be a father is learning how to adjust to this new, suddenly expanding world – a world that includes your family and friends and your partner's family and friends. While some people are stepping back, others are coming forward in your life. Some changes have already occurred, with plenty more to come. And all of this is occurring because of a tiny little being you haven't even met yet.

Chapter 6

Common Fears

Pregnancy is a physical and emotional experience for women. But for men, after they help create the baby, there is no physical side. The growth they experience is psychological. This chapter discusses some emotional and mental hurdles that men must deal with on the road to fatherhood.

Your Feelings Are Normal

The variety of emotions that most fathers-to-be experience are normal and natural. Every man feels a variety of emotions during pregnancy, and there is nothing wrong with this. It is just part of being human.

Still, many fathers-to-be do not like to admit that they feel doubt or worry or fear about what lies ahead. There are good reasons for this reluctance. Men intuitively understand that their job during pregnancy is different from their partner's. They know that a lot of unnecessary emotion on their part is not going to help them do that job.

Men need to be steady and solid and reliable during this time of change. The father-to-be wants to be the cool, calm man in a crisis; he needs to be there for his partner and come through for her; he also knows, because it is true, that what he *feels* at this time is not nearly as important as what he *does*.

This is another reason that men shy away from admitting they even have the feelings they have, let alone expressing them. The father-to-be's 'issues', if you want to call them that, are indeed secondary to his partner's and the baby's, and the man knows that. For many men, having any doubts or worries at all seems like a kind of betrayal. It feels like an admission of weakness, a sign that they may not be up to the job they are supposed to do and that they sincerely want to do. They are embarrassed to have these feelings and do not like talking about them.

One could argue, however, that feelings such as doubt, worry and even fear are a sign that you are preparing yourself emotionally for the job ahead. Accepting and understanding your feelings may help you do a better job as a father, not a worse one. It may also help to know that virtually every father before you has experienced feelings similar to yours. But they made it, and so can you.

Passing Out in the Delivery Room

Many popular sitcoms on television feature scenes that take place in a hospital delivery room, with women in labour and babies being born.

You can decrease your worries about fainting in the delivery room (if you have any) by taking childbirth preparation classes with your partner. Also talk to other fathers: the simple fact that other men you know have gone through it and not encountered any problems will be reassuring to you.

Frequently the hapless fathers-to-be are shown as bumbling fools who faint during childbirth. Another running joke is the father-to-be forgetting what he needs to do when his partner goes into labour. These fathers run around like idiots before jumping in the car and screeching off to the hospital. When they arrive, someone has to point out that they have forgotten to bring the person who is actually having the baby, and they sheepishly climb back in the car to go and get their wives.

Even today, the man-who-faints-during-childbirth bit is still a popular comedy staple. However, despite its popularity in comedy, it almost never happens in real life. You would have to hunt far and wide to find an obstetrician or midwife who has actually seen the father pass out in the delivery room.

Not Being Able to Provide

There is a sound and sensible reason for fathers-to-be to worry during pregnancy. There are things to worry about. With the possible exception of passing out in the delivery room, these worries are not just in your head or media fictions. They are grounded in objective reality.

With a baby on the way, even early on in pregnancy, certain things need to be done. If they are not done, well, that can cause problems. And one of the chief worries for both expectant fathers and mothers is, not to beat about the bush, money.

Doing the Financial Sums

You don't have to be a genius to work any of this out. Just do the maths. When there was just you and your partner, you had two incomes supporting two people. When a baby enters the picture, you will have two incomes supporting three people.

But wait a second – somebody is going to have to take care of that baby. Either you will have to pay for childcare, which is certainly not cheap, or one of you will have to stay home. That somebody, almost always, is the mother. How long she stays off work is a thorny question, and the answer varies from family to family. But she will probably be off work for at least several months. This may well reduce her income, which will change the financial picture once more.

Instead of having two incomes supporting two people, you now have one income – probably yours – supporting three people. No wonder you're worried. It is the most reasonable thing in the world for a man to have concerns during this time about supporting his family.

Expectant parents worry about money because it directly affects how much time they will be able to spend with their child. This holds true for both women and men. One survey found that 65 per cent of all fathers said they would spend more time with their children if they could afford to do so.

The Emotional Nature of Money

A certain amount of worry can be beneficial to some degree. It may be an indication that you need to take action in a given area. But too much worry may hurt you, perhaps even prevent you from acting. All this is complicated – made more troublesome, if you will – by the emotional nature of money.

Some people will say money is merely a matter of pounds and pence, strictly a bottom-line issue. While this may be true when you are running a business, it is seldom the case with a family. This is particularly true when you have a baby because how you feel about money is so often connected to your own (and your partner's) childhood and upbringing. For instance, if you didn't have much material comfort when you were growing up, you may be determined to give your child what you never had, even if you can't always afford to.

There are practical steps you can take to ease your worries over money. They require some advance planning, perhaps some hard thinking that may force some hard choices, and a sit-down or two with your partner to talk it all over. These steps are all discussed in greater detail in Chapters 7, 8 and 9.

Is It Really My Child?

One of the things that many men think about is whether or not the child is actually theirs. Are they the father? Although many men wonder this, few talk about their worry openly. It's just something that gnaws at the pit of their stomach.

In most cases, this is a baseless worry. Intellectually, you know that you are, of course, the father. This is, once more, a reminder of how different it is to be a father than a mother. There can be no doubt who the mother is; the baby is growing inside her. But Dad? Sometimes even after the baby is born, and her physical characteristics resemble the father's, some men continue to have doubts.

While a father-to-be might have these worries, he is probably also insulted by the very idea that his partner could have had an affair. He does not believe the woman carrying his child has been cheating, and the very idea of it hurts. More likely, his worry stems from the fact that many men are simply overwhelmed by the idea that they helped create a baby, that they participated in something so monumental as to cause another human being to be born. This causes them to doubt themselves and their own child's paternity.

Ageing and Mortality

Having a baby can bring out issues in your life that maybe you have ignored or been in denial about for a period of time. One of those issues is your age. Suddenly, with a baby on the way, you feel a lot older than you did only months ago. Why should this be the case? Part of it has to do with the fact that your role in life is changing radically, and with this change you are being forced to look at yourself – and everything about you – in a new way.

From Son to Father

All your life you have been somebody's son. Being a son implies youth, starting out on life's journey, and to a certain degree, being protected by your parents. While you are still a son to your parents, with the coming arrival of your own child you are also taking on a new role – that of father. Being a father has different associations, and it comes with different responsibilities.

The man who has become a father has, without doubt, greater duties than the man who is a son. The father must provide for his family. He must sacrifice his own desires to their desires and needs. He is a teacher, a disciplinarian and a role model.

One of the most obvious differences between a father and a son is age. When you are a son, you hardly think about time because you feel you have so much of it, so much that you can waste it. The father has a different view. He has lived in the world a little bit and absorbed its hard knocks. For him, time is in short supply. It is too precious to waste.

A Sense of Mortality

These thoughts and feelings about age and growing older occur naturally to every man when he is about to become a father. After the baby comes, these feelings only intensify, in part because they reflect reality. Each birthday the baby celebrates means that not only is he another year older, but you are too. Time speeds up when you become a parent.

Your child now occupies your former position – the young, protected one who is just beginning life's journey. Your role has switched to that of provider, protector, teacher and role model. If somebody has to make a sacrifice for the betterment of the family, it is going to be you (or your partner) who has to bite the bullet and do it.

Your own parents may or may not be living. Whatever the case, in becoming a father, you have a changed view of your own mortality. Before, as a son, your own father or parents stood between you and the ultimate mystery. In the natural order of things – although things, of course, do not always follow this order – they would die before you. This was only one of the ways in which you felt protected by them.

But with a child on the way, the old order is being rearranged. It's like the children's game of musical chairs. Your baby has taken your former chair, and you have moved into a chair that signifies that you are one step closer to being done with the game. It's a sobering realization.

Is something wrong with me if I don't have these feelings?
Not at all. Some men feel these issues strongly, while others hardly ever think about them, and then only in passing. Each man's experience of fatherhood is unique to him, at the same time that many of these experiences and feelings are universal.

Becoming like Dad

When you become a parent (or a parent-to-be), you will receive a large amount of advice from many well-meaning people – friends, family and sometimes even complete strangers. You will listen to the doctors and medical specialists. You will read books and attend childbirth preparation classes. But the biggest influence on how you will bring up your children is already part of your psyche.

How were you brought up as a child? What was it like when you were growing up? How did your parents handle things? All your childhood issues, whatever they are, will resurface when you become a parent. This will also hold true for your partner, who is likely to be grappling with similar issues relating to her own childhood and parents.

Your chief role model for being a father was your own father. You learned lessons from him on how to be a man and a father, whether you are conscious of these lessons or not. Some of these lessons may be bad, some good. But you must be prepared to deal with them when you yourself become a father.

The Bad Father

Let's face it. Not all dads are good role models. After he retired from playing American football, former Chicago Bears middle linebacker Mike Singletary became active in religion and promoting responsibility among men. One day he went to a women's prison to speak. The warden warned him to expect an unfriendly reception from the female inmates. 'Why is that?' Singletary asked. 'Because you're a man and a father', said the warden, 'and in almost every case, the one person who has caused the most pain in all of these inmates' lives is their father.'

Some fathers do bad things to their children and their partners. Some desert their families. Some cause so much trouble and misery that it is better for everyone involved if they simply leave the house and never come back so that the mother can get on with bringing up the children without their interference.

Your father may have done some terrible things to you, both knowingly and unconsciously. And in the back of your mind, you may be thinking, 'Does that mean I'm going to do rotten things too? Is that what it means to be a father – never to be around, and then on those few times when you're around, to scold your children constantly and cause misery? Am I going to be like him?'

The Good Father

The opposite role model is the good father. This is the man who has always acted for the good of his family. In the popular view of films and television, the good father is strong but caring, a thoughtful, patient person who dispenses nuggets of wisdom to his children that they carry with them for the rest of their lives.

You may have a dad somewhat like this – a man you looked up to, perhaps even idolized. But just because he was such a great role model, you may think to yourself, 'How can I ever be as good a father? How can I ever live up to the standards he set?' And these sorts of thoughts may make you uneasy.

Becoming Your Own Man

Like the bad father, the good father may only exist in your memory or perception. The reality may be that your father had both good and bad points. He was a flawed man, perhaps, who made mistakes but did the best he could for his family, given his circumstances and the times in which he lived. Remember that your own dad, for all his faults, was once an adult man, like yourself, who had to make the transition into fatherhood. His own father (and mother) may not have been the greatest role models in the world either.

When you become a parent, you hopefully will become more sympathetic and understanding of your own parents. You realize what a hard job they had. It's impossible to do or say the right thing at every given moment with your children. Nevertheless, it is important to recognize that when you become a father, you *can* follow your own path and make your own choices.

Be aware. Make conscious choices. Check your motives to make sure you are acting because you truly think what you are doing is the right thing. Some parents-to-be think things should be done a certain way simply because that is how it was done when they were children.

Will My Relationship Be Hurt?

Both men and women worry about how a baby will affect their relationship. For this reason, many couples put off getting pregnant for many years. They do not want a child to affect what they have together as a couple or all the things they want to do.

As the divorce rates show, these worries are anything but groundless. A child puts stress on a relationship. Here are only a few of the stresses that come with having a child:

· Less free time	· Less time for anything but the baby
· Less romantic time	· More money worries
· More exhaustion	· More in-law involvement
· More demands on you	· More potential sources of disagreement

It is possible that just your partner's becoming pregnant has added new friction points to your relationship that were not there before. You may have already noticed that you have less free time because you feel the need to get home to tend to your partner's needs. Your in-laws may be calling and coming over more. Other stresses may be popping up. What you are feeling will only increase once the baby arrives.

Concerns about Your Partner

Labour and delivery are not without risk. That is why most couples choose to give birth in a hospital. If something unexpected happens to either mother or child, they are surrounded by medical professionals who can give them immediate attention. Lives may truly hang in the balance.

For men, another aspect of the process is watching their partner endure so much pain for so long. It is difficult to see the woman you love go through such great hardship, and there is little you can do about it except encourage her verbally and moisten her forehead with a wet flannel or give her a back rub. Women giving birth have also been known to single out the person who got them into this position – um, that's you – and subject him to a terrible tongue-lashing, screaming and swearing at him in language that would embarrass a sailor. While this doesn't happen often, it certainly has been known to occur.

This is hard to take – seeing your partner in so much pain and hearing her swear at you. Even so, men realize that their burden is far, far, far lighter than the one being carried by the woman. If it were somehow magically possible for fathers to swap places with mothers, letting them carry a baby to term and then give birth, most men would politely but respectfully decline the offer.

Concerns about the Baby

Again, as with so many of the other worries and fears discussed in this chapter, there is a reason to be concerned about your baby. It's possible that something could go wrong. That is why you and your partner are learning everything you can about this event, and why so many trained people – doctors, midwives, specialists – are involved in helping it happen safely.

> By about the third month, the foetus has fingers and toes with soft nails. By the next month, she has fingerprints and toe prints. By the sixth month her movements have become strong and coordinated, and her hands sometimes grip the umbilical cord. Six months is also about the time when a baby can survive outside her mother's body in intensive care.

You can also feel reassured by the many medical tests and screens that your partner is undergoing. Still, even with all these procedures (which are not 100 per cent foolproof), you may worry that your child will not turn out 'normal' in some way. When no one is looking, many new fathers count their child's toes and fingers once he's born to make sure he has them all.

Getting Support

Your concerns about your partner and your child are not just in your head. You need not feel ashamed of them. They are not a sign of weakness. Every father-to-be feels these things. In the same way, the doubts you may have about yourself are similar to what other fathers-to-be are feeling and what other fathers before you have felt when they went through this process.

Even if they're chewing their fingernails off with worry, many men do not want to admit that they are experiencing doubts or worries about the pregnancy. Even if they will confess to a niggling doubt or two, they reckon they can handle it on their own without asking for help. This may be true. You may not need a shoulder to lean on. But if you do, there are places where you can find support.

Finding a Sympathetic Ear

One good place to start is with somebody who has been through it before – your brother, perhaps, or a close friend. He may make a joke at the start because revealing his feelings puts him in a vulnerable position too. But once he sees that you're serious and willing to open up to him, he will almost certainly let down his guard as well.

It may not be necessary for this person to be a father or, for that matter, another man. You may have a close woman friend and feel more comfortable talking to her. Many men find it easier to talk to women because they tend to listen better and do not feel the need to tell you what to do or immediately offer solutions.

Men's Support Groups

You may be more comfortable talking to people you don't know all that well, such as a men's support group that meets at a church or local community centre. These men have probably gone through what you're going through, and they will be sympathetic to what you are experiencing.

When you receive advice or information, always consider the source. Whether the advice is from your father, a friend or an anonymous person on the Internet, the advice that people give is nearly always a reflection of themselves and their own experiences. Just because something worked for them does not necessarily mean it will work for you.

Another possible avenue is a chat room on the Internet. There are numerous chat rooms for fathers on websites devoted to parenting. On the Internet, you truly can get some things off your chest without anyone having to know who you are.

Professional Help

If you feel overwhelmed or troubled by your impending fatherhood, why not talk to a professional about it? There is no harm in seeking advice, and it may help. You can talk to a professional therapist or your priest or minister. Your talk will be considered private, and you will be sure of getting a sympathetic ear.

The great thing about talking about these concerns is that the talk alone may prove therapeutic. Because you are dealing with emotions, there may be no specific solution to your given concern. But you feel better simply because you got to talk about it.

Talking to Your Partner

Surely the best person to confide in is your partner, the mother of your child. But she may be so wrapped up with the child inside her that she hasn't really thought about you. She may be surprised that you have such feelings. At first she may even be dismissive of your concerns and feel that you are being selfish and thinking only of yourself.

If this occurs, ask for a time when you can both talk. Let her talk fully, and when she is done, take your turn. She may be more willing to listen to you once she feels her concerns have been heard.

Of course, it is highly possible that your partner is genuinely interested in your interior life. She may be secretly concerned about you. She may feel you drifting away from her emotionally and wonder if you are having second thoughts about the whole situation. The chance to talk may relieve her greatly and give peace of mind to you both.

Fatherhood is a new experience, and so are many of the questions that come with the territory. But these thoughts are all part of the process of becoming a father.

Chapter 7

The Economics of Having a Baby

Money is a prime concern for couples expecting a new baby. It can cause arguments and stress. This chapter covers the basics of money management. It includes topics like why it is important to set family priorities, the credit traps you need to avoid, and strategies you can use to reduce your worries and increase your sense of security.

Money Worries

It has been said that the arguments between couples tend to focus on two main areas: sex and money. Sex will be discussed in Chapter 11. As for money, it is certainly understandable that cash would be something both men and women would worry and occasionally argue about during this sensitive time. The economics of having a baby can seem awfully scary; indeed, that is why many couples put off becoming parents in the first place. They feel they cannot afford it.

You and your partner have probably been paying the bills on two incomes, yours and hers. With a baby on the way, you are looking ahead to the time when your partner will stop working for an undetermined period both before and after the birth. That means that the three of you will probably find yourselves living on your income alone, at least for a few months.

The Mother's point of view

In Chapter 9, you will learn ways that you and your partner can soften the financial blow during this time. She may be entitled to maternity pay when she goes on leave from her job. While she is off, she may in addition have some holiday pay entitlement, depending on her company's or organization's policies and how long she has worked there. You may also be able to draw from personal savings.

All this will help, but it may not entirely ease her mind. She may have worked and collected a pay cheque every week of her adult life since leaving school. But now that she's pregnant, she's in a more vulnerable position than she's been in for a long time. She knows she will not be in work for a while, and that during this period she will be caring for the baby. To some degree, depending on how you two have worked things out, she may be dependent on you financially.

Your Point of View

As much as you'd like to reassure her on this score, you have worries of your own. In fact, you may even have lost sleep over it. You've done the mathematics and number-crunching over and over in your head, and you've come to the conclusion that you just can't do it. There is simply no way that you can afford to have a baby at this time.

But it's too late. The baby's on the way, and there's no turning back. You think about ways that you can make more money. Ask for a rise? No way, you're not due for a salary review until next year.

What about looking for a better-paid job? That's a possibility, but it takes time. Get a second job? That's another option. Many fathers and fathers-to-be do indeed work longer hours and get second jobs so they can make more money to provide for their families.

According to research published in October 2002 by the Equal Opportunities Commission (EOC), although fathers play a range of roles in the family, most still see themselves mainly as breadwinner. This is partly due to women's lower average pay, and also men's lack of confidence in their own caring skills combined with a working culture of long and inflexible hours.

The Way It Goes

It may be reassuring to know that practically every other father-to-be in the world worries about money. And unless you've got a million in the bank, it is reasonable to have such concerns. You worry about financial stability just as you worry about the health of your child and partner.

But nobody has a handle on these issues right away. They take time to work out. You may not have every detail completely planned before the birth. When the baby finally arrives, new issues will pop up that you hadn't planned on. Expect to feel financial pressures for as long as you are bringing up children.

Money: It's a Family Affair

One thing to realize is that the money burden is not all on your shoulders. Even if you make more money than she does, even if you are the chief provider and feel strongly in your heart that this is your most important role and the way that you can best contribute to your family's well-being, finances are a shared responsibility, and you and your partner need to face these issues together.

Look at it this way. You're sharing more of the household chores, right? You're cooking more, doing some of the food shopping. You're going with your partner to her antenatal appointments and planning to be at the birth. And when the baby comes home, you're going to be elbow to elbow with your partner, changing nappies, mixing bottles and doing whatever needs to be done. Your partner can share some of the financial responsibilities in the same way as you're helping out in these areas.

She is thinking a lot about money issues too. She's got her own set of worries. Which means that she may be willing to sit down with you at the kitchen table and talk.

Your partner may be focused inwardly on the baby and not be thinking about money as much as you are. Talking about it may initially scare or intimidate her. She may feel defensive. Reassure her by explaining that you simply feel the need to confer with her and stay in sync on this important subject that concerns you both.

The Emotions of Money

It is customary for financial experts to talk about money as if it is merely a matter of pounds and pence. While this may be true when you are preparing a profit-and-loss statement for a business, it is definitely not the case when you are dealing with families, especially families with a baby on the way. Emotions come into play. This is why working out household finances can sometimes be such a thorny affair – there are so many more issues to deal with than just money alone.

How You Were Brought Up

When you have a baby, your own childhood and the way you were brought up will greatly influence how you act as a parent. Did you grow up with plenty, or was there a feeling that there was never enough? Were your parents fair? Did they play favourites with you or any of your brothers and sisters?

Perhaps you were an only child. Because of this, you may want to have only one child yourself. Of course, the reverse may also be true. Because you never had a brother or sister, you may want to have a big family so your children will have siblings.

If you did not have something as a child, you may feel strongly that you must give this thing you lacked to your child. This could be virtually anything: money, toys, a big house, a private education, love. Or because you had a rich abundance as a child, you may be determined to provide the same bounty to your offspring.

How Your Partner Was Brought Up

You bring a certain amount of emotional baggage into parenthood. So does your partner – and her baggage isn't the same as yours. Always try to bear this in mind when you talk with her about money. You both may work up a great deal of emotional heat on topics that, from a strictly financial point of view, are relatively unimportant. But these issues lie at the core of how you see yourself as a parent and your expectations for your child.

Your partner had her own unique childhood experiences. These experiences, whether good or bad, will help shape her view about how money should be spent, just as your childhood informs your view. Here are some other non-pounds-and-pence issues that are likely to come up in your discussions:

- Your values – what you believe is right for your child.
- Your expectations – what you expect to happen.
- Your image of parenthood – what it is supposed to be like.
- Your partner's view of your role as father, and your view of her as mother.
- Peer pressure – what other parents do with their children.
- Family pressure – what your parents or other family members think should happen.

Some of the expectations you have about raising children are formed out of your own experience. Other people's experiences and what they have told you will also play a role. Television programmes and the media may have led you to create some unrealistic expectations of what family life is like. All this will emerge when you talk about the often emotionally volatile subject of money.

Setting Your Priorities

There are no easy answers to all these money questions, and every family works out financial issues in its own way. What works for one family may not work for another. But every family establishes priorities, and these priorities determine how they spend their money.

You may never have talked to your partner about your financial priorities. Nevertheless, both of you demonstrate your priorities every day without saying a word to each other or anyone else. At the end of each month, take a look at how you spent your money. That will tell you all about what your priorities are.

What can be upsetting about learning that you are about to become a father is the discovery that you may have to change your spending priorities. In some cases, a minor adjustment may not be enough; or perhaps your habits need a complete overhaul. Your partner may feel the same way. Something has got to change – or else.

Strategies for Getting Money

Stripped of emotion (which is, admittedly, a very hard thing to do), the economics of pregnancy are like the economics of everyday life. Quite simply, you need to make more money than you spend. If you are not able to do this – and many new parents are not – you need to find ways to cover the shortfall. There are a variety of methods you can use to help.

Use the Resources You Have

As mentioned earlier, many fathers-to-be and fathers take second jobs to build up their savings or pay off bills. Another form of 'saving' is to start piling up paid holiday entitlement at work that you can use after the baby is born. Both you and your wife can do this.

Do you own your home? You may be able to take out a second mortgage that will supply you with cash. Be careful if you are considering going down this route, however – your home is your greatest financial asset, now and in the future. When you decide to take out a second mortgage you are, in effect, selling a long-term asset for short-term reasons. But your partner may really want to stay at home with the baby for a certain amount of time, and you may decide that this particular trade-off is worth it.

Be financially cautious during the pregnancy. Do not make any big spending or investment decisions. You have enough things on your mind as it is. After the baby comes and you get settled into this new life, then you can review your overall financial picture and see what needs to be done to improve it.

Another possibility is to sell something of value, such as that classic car or motorbike gathering dust in the garage or under a tarpaulin in the driveway. If you have a resource like this and are willing to part with it, it is another way to produce extra cash until your partner goes back to work and finances are on a more even keel.

Borrowing or Receiving Money as a Gift

Your parents or your wife's parents may be able to help you financially. They may even offer to help without your asking. They know the financial pressures you're under because they themselves faced similar pressures when they were new parents. And they've come to a point in their lives at which they are better able to help their children and grandchildren.

If they cannot afford to give you money, they may be willing to give you a short-term loan. This is better than borrowing money from a bank, getting a cash advance on your credit card or taking out a second mortgage. All those loans you must pay back with interest. Even if your parents charge you interest, it will be nothing like the terms a bank will demand. And if you have trouble paying the money back on time, your family is not going to send in the bailiffs or repossess your house.

Pride may stop you from asking for or accepting money from your parents or relatives. You also may not want them to get tangled up in your financial affairs, and their gift or loan may come with strings attached. As always, you will need to weigh the cost of receiving this money against the advantages that come from taking it.

Credit Card Debt

It is going to be difficult to get ahead financially if you carry exorbitant credit card debt. The more debt you incur, the bigger the hole you are digging for yourself. When you pay that interest fee to the bank every month to service that debt, it is like throwing money away – and putting more dirt in the hole that you must ultimately dig out.

Dispose of all your credit and store cards, and get rid of your bank overdraft facility. These cost money unless you always pay your monthly account in full and on time. Then you won't be able to buy things you can't afford. If you cannot face this option, then look for a card with the lowest available interest rate and free balance transfers. Visit the website www.moneysupermarket.com, where you can compare the rates of more than 300 credit cards.

New parents generally understand this, but again, the emotions come into play. Your partner's dream may be to have the perfect little nursery. In her mind, this requires a total makeover of the baby's room – new crib, new furniture, new paint job, new everything. You don't have the money to pay for it, so you pull out the plastic.

Baby Expenses

Babies don't require very much equipment to begin with. A lot of things can be borrowed or bought secondhand – although the experts say that car seats should, ideally, be purchased new. Here is a list of what you will want in the house before the baby arrives. Anything else can wait.

· Enough nappies to keep you going for at least the first few days or so – at least 50 disposables. If you are planning to use cotton nappies, keep an emergency stock of Pampers handy too.
· A changing mat, or changing unit and baby wipes or cotton wool.
· Three or four all-in-one sleepsuits.
· At least three or four vests, also known as body suits, with envelope necks and poppers underneath. These can be worn under babygros, or on their own when it is very hot.
· One or two blankets to wrap your baby in.
· One or two cardigans to provide an extra layer.
· For winter babies, an all-in-one warm suit.
· Moses basket, cot or crib.
· Cot sheets and cellular blankets, or a bottom sheet and a baby sleeping bag.
· A baby bath (or you can use a washing up bowl), or a newborn bath support.
· A couple of small towels.
· A rear-facing car seat, if your baby will be travelling by car.
· A pram, pushchair or buggy suitable for newborns – with a lie-flat position).
· Nursing bras and breast pads if your partner plans to breastfeed.
· Bottles, teats, bottle brushes and sterilizer (microwave ones are ideal), if you intend to bottle feed.

For more information on buying for your new baby, visit the excellent website at www.babycentre.co.uk.

Getting Help

Having a baby does not need to bankrupt you. Think twice before going into debt to buy a whole lot of new stuff. If you do, you are doing a disservice both to your child and yourself. You are going to have to pay for those things at some point. This will force you to spend more time working, so you will have less time with your family as a result.

Having a child brings up lots of emotions. If you and your partner can discuss and deal with some of these emotional issues, you may not need to run up your credit card bills. Remember, you're spending this money on a little person you've never met, who, frankly, does not care if she gets changed on a brand-new deluxe changing table or a towel laid out on the bed. But money is a complicated topic for lots of reasons, and everyone needs help from time to time.

Financial Advice

It may make sense for you to seek financial advice. Independent financial advisers (IFAs) must by law give you unbiased advice that best suits your personal requirements. Your bank or building society may offer independent financial advice; or they may simply sell their own financial products. Some solicitors and accountants offer independent financial advice; while most insurance company advisers sell only their own products. 'Free' financial advisers are paid on commission, earning a percentage of the money you invest. This can lead them to point you in the direction of specific products. If you choose a fee-based adviser (who charges for the hours worked), the chances are you'll get unbiased advice.

A financial adviser can review your situation and provide counsel on both your immediate present as well as the future. He or she may look critically at how you spend your money, and may give you advice as simple as shifting funds from a bank account to a higher interest savings account. He or she will almost certainly talk to you about investing for your and your child's future. For more on investing strategies, refer to Chapter 8.

Credit Counselling

It is as hard to change long-time spending habits as it is to stop smoking or drinking. And with both you and your partner earning good salaries, there may have been no reason to change. Everything may have been going fine until she got pregnant and you both had to take a hard look at how you were going to swing this whole deal, money-wise. You may have come to the realization that you are digging a hole for yourself and the hole is only getting deeper.

You may have lost your job and forgotten to plan for your partner's loss of income during pregnancy. You may have underestimated the costs involved in buying for a baby. Any or all of these things could have happened, causing you to go thousands of pounds in debt.

Don't pay for debt counselling: it's free from the Citizens Advice Bureau, or they can refer you to a money expert if necessary. Various organizations give debt advice, including some charities, government bodies or church-sponsored organizations such as Credit Action. You can also get help online from the National Debtline at www.nationaldebtline. co.uk or the Citizens Advice Bureau at www.adviceguide.org.uk.

Every couple worries about money when they are about to have a baby. These worries can trigger intense emotions, emotions that touch on your image of yourself as a parent and your expectations for you and your child. Realizing this, you and your partner need to talk about your priorities and values. Once you are clear about what comes first, the question of what you need to do with your money – whether to spend less, pay off debt or save more – will become much clearer, too.

Chapter 8

Long-Term Financial Issues

When you become a father, you need to think both short- and long-term. You need adequate income for the immediate present, but you cannot completely ignore the future – yours or your family's. Here are some financial planning issues to think about for the months ahead.

Why Your Perspective Is Valuable

Sometimes men feel left out of their partner's pregnancy. All the focus is on her and the baby. They're not sure how they fit in or how they can be useful. One of the ways you can be useful is to do some thinking and planning about money.

Your partner may be a planner at heart. The two of you may have already sat down at the kitchen table, calculator in hand. Maybe you've already printed out your spending and income statements for the year. Your pencils may be worn to the nub from plotting out your financial situation for the next year. The chances are, however, that she is a little distracted with this baby growing bigger and bigger inside her, and she has many things on her mind besides money.

This is where you may be able to take the wheel and let her relax for a while. Your perspective on spending and finances is valuable. She will almost certainly welcome your ability to take the lead on these issues. It means one less thing she has to think about.

Always keep talking with your partner – about money and everything else. This is the wrong time to make any big decisions on spending or a job without first consulting her. Just as you want to stay in tune with her pregnancy, keep her involved in your thinking and decision-making.

Buying a Bigger Vehicle

One of the things that happens when you learn you are going to be a father is that you look around at all the things in your life and realize how inadequate they are. What worked for two people is clearly not going to make it for three, especially when that third person is a baby. Baby changes everything, or so you think.

Your car may become a sudden source of consternation. You love that sporty little two-seater, but where are you going to put the baby? And your partner's old runabout is ready to be put out to pasture. Does becoming a father mean you have to buy a people carrier?

The Family Monster-Mobile

If you have ever ventured into the vicinity of an infants' or junior school when all the parents are arriving to pick up their children, you might think that in order to have a family these days, it is required that you own a sport utility vehicle or 4WD. It can be comical to watch tiny three and four-year-olds who can't tie their shoelaces get strapped into the car seat of a giant off-roader. These vehicles are as big as a house on wheels, and yet it is only Mum and child roaring down the road together to ballet or football practice.

Sport utility vehicles have become the ride of choice for many families, partly because of their roominess and the feeling of safety and security they provide. Another aspect of their appeal is their image as a rugged, outdoorsy, off-road vehicle. Men in particular seem to like this, although only a tiny percentage of SUV owners ever travel on anything but paved streets. Men also like being able to sit up high in a SUV, which allows them to see the road better.

The People Carrier

Another popular family-mobile is the people carrier, which is also a common sight wherever parents and children congregate. It was all the rage some years ago, until it developed image problems. Because of the dowdy image, car makers have designed sleeker, more stylish people carriers that they hope will appeal to dads as well as mums.

In a similar attempt to broaden the appeal of sport utility vehicles, manufacturers have developed smoother-riding SUVs and 'mini-SUVs' with the feel and handling more of a car than a lorry. What attracts families to both people carriers and SUVs is obvious: lots of room inside to carry children.

Your Parents' Family-Mobile

One more option to consider in terms of a family vehicle is an estate car. Like the people carrier, it has suffered in popularity because of image problems. Many baby boomers had parents who drove a Vauxhall estate or another type of estate car. When the baby boomers grew up and became parents themselves, they did not want to drive what their mother and father did. Out went the big estate, in came the people carrier and SUV. Nevertheless, an estate car offers more space than a saloon or hatchback, and often as much as an SUV, which can be deceptively small inside compared against how big it looks on the outside. The open boxed area at the back that make SUVs and some people carriers so popular is the traditional selling point of an estate car – and the latter often have far more space than SUVs or people carriers.

No Need to Buy Anything Now

Now that you are about to become a family man, one of these large vehicles may be in your future. But that doesn't mean you have to get rid of that zippy little convertible just yet.

However you work it out, one thing is sure. You do not need to buy a new car yet (unless you drive a Smart car, in which case you will have to start thinking). Babies are small – yours will almost certainly fit just fine into a car seat in the back seat of your current car. As time passes and you get a better sense of what you need and can afford, then you can think about perhaps getting a more family-friendly set of wheels.

Before buying a car, think about your priorities. Do you want to add monthly car payments to your bills on top of everything else? If you've got the money to swing it financially, more power to you. But given all the uncertainties that come with pregnancy and children, it is wiser to wait.

Owning a Home

For most people, buying a house is the biggest financial investment they will ever make. Given today's house prices, they will probably take on large amounts of debt and pay a sizable monthly mortgage along with council tax. But unlike paying rent to a landlord, the house you buy will probably increase in value over the years, making your investment a sound one.

But a house is more than just a financial asset or an investment; it is where you live, and where you are going to bring up your children. Buying a home means that you are putting down roots in a community. It has psychological and spiritual significance. You are planting a flag, claiming this place as your own.

Home as Nest

The pressure to buy a house sometimes starts with pregnancy. You and your partner may be content living in a flat. But with a baby on the way, loft-style living no longer seems appropriate. You feel the need to get more space, perhaps to have a garden.

Many couples put off having a child until they can get into a house of their own. The reason for this often has to do with people's memories of childhood – how they were brought up. They grew up in a house, not in a flat, and they want the same for their children.

Many fathers-to-be notice that their partners develop a nesting instinct when they become pregnant. They want a safe, secure place to have their baby. Security, in their minds, often equates with living in a house.

A Complicated and Expensive Decision

To buy a house, first you need to come up with a down payment. This normally equals about 25 per cent of the purchase price of the home, but many lenders will loan up to 90 or even 95 per cent of the property's value. Some will even let you have up to 100 per cent – but this can be expensive and you will probably have to buy mortgage indemnity insurance as a condition of the mortgage.

The amount you can borrow varies between lenders, but the rule of thumb is three times your annual earnings – although sometimes people are lent five times their income. More important is, how much can you afford? Some lenders will want to look at your average outgoings (household bills, debts and so forth); others will ask you to respond to a detailed questionnaire. First-time buyers benefit from showing they've been paying regular rent for a similar amount to their intended mortgage payments. Visit the website www.mortgagesorter.co.uk for answers to most mortgage questions and 'best buy' tables.

Balancing Your Priorities

To find an affordable place to buy, many families buy a home far away from where they work. This increases their commute and keeps them away from their family longer during the day. Many fathers (and mothers) must get up early in the morning and leave for work before their children wake up. The only time they see them is in the evening.

A house is a worthwhile investment for both family and financial reasons. But again, it's a matter of balancing your priorities. The increased financial demands of home ownership may force you and your partner to put your child in day care for much of the day. But you may feel this is worth it because you love your home and community, and your child will be going to good schools and live in an area with lots of other children around.

Generally, the financial burdens of raising children are most acute when children are in their younger years. As they grow older, some of these pressures ease. Your partner may also return to her job. Additionally, your income may grow over the years as your career develops. All of this will tend to give you more flexibility and the ability to take on more financial responsibility.

Life Insurance

Every man is different, but chances are you do not have life insurance. After all, why should you? Until now it's just been you and your partner. You work; she works. If something happened to you, she has an income and she could take care of herself.

But this equation changes with the arrival of a baby. Now you have somebody else to think about, a tiny baby who depends on you for his care. What would happen to him if something bad happened to you?

Thoughts of Mortality

What a drag, right? Here you are, about to have a baby, one of the most life-affirming events in all creation, and you've got to think about... your demise. This whole business of dying is only hypothetical, though, which is why some men can't stand the idea of paying for life insurance. They feel like they're throwing money away.

That is certainly a truism about life insurance – you hope no one ever has to collect on your policy. But nobody has a crystal ball, and you never know what the future holds. That's why you take out life insurance, because anything can happen.

Your Partner May Need Protection, Too

Money may be tight, and you may already be having a hard time paying the bills without forking out for an annual life insurance premium. But remember the situation you're in. Baby is on the way, and your partner is about to take some time off work. She plans to return to her job as soon as she can, but perhaps only on a part-time basis at first because you both agree that she needs to devote as much time as possible to caring for the baby. Now, what if suddenly your income wasn't available?

If your partner has an income, you need to think about getting some cover for her, too. The theory behind life insurance is to help the survivors continue to live more or less as they have been, without being forced to move or to suffer major disruptions because of financial hardship. This applies to women as well. If something happened to your partner, it might be tough for you alone to make up for the loss of her income.

Life insurance pays your partner a lump sum if you die. 'Term life insurance' lasts for a specific time and may be linked to your mortgage; the 'term' is usually 25 years. 'Whole life cover' is an insurance designed to last until you die. When you take out life insurance you should ensure the amount the policy would pay your partner is enough to cover her living expenses, the cost of your funeral (surprisingly expensive), childcare and so forth.

Making a Will

Another thing that you and your partner need to do is write a will. If you die before making a will (the legal term is 'intestate'), your partner may lose control of what happens to your estate (house, car, possessions) because court administrators will sort out your affairs. Making a will is pretty straightforward, and if your finances are simple, you won't even need a solicitor. Many people choose to buy software specially designed for making a will or write their wills online. Go to www.lawpack.co.uk or www.desktoplawyer.co.uk, or in Scotland www.scotwills.co.uk for further information.

It's worth using a solicitor if your estate is very complex or you have very specific and detailed bequests. You also need professional advice if you have children from an earlier marriage, or if you are responsible for caring for someone with mental or physical disabilities. And anyone who has their own business, or whose assets exceed the inheritance tax threshold (£275,000 in 2005–6) should consult a solicitor when drawing up their will.

Saving for Education

One of the most intimidating aspects of having children is the idea of paying for their future university or college education. The sums needed to go on to further education today are astronomical. Projections of what students will have to pay 18 years from now – when your child may be a first-year student – are even more daunting. Unless you have a gold mine in your back garden, how on earth can you expect to come up with that kind of money?

If you are already thinking about saving and investing for further education, you are to be commended for your foresight. Many fathers-to-be and fathers would prefer not to think about it at all. However, setting aside even small amounts of money each week or month as from today is a great way to start.

You may be pleasantly surprised at how quickly money saved in this way grows (visit the website www.thisismoney.co.uk and click on 'tools and calculators' to work out how your savings might increase in value).

Even if your child chooses not to go to university, you'll probably have saved enough money to put down as a deposit on his or her first flat.

Savings bonds or other policies to be used for further education make great gifts from parents or in-laws. Everybody is a winner on that one.

Thinking about Retirement

Retirement is another of those down-the-road topics that may not feel immediately relevant to you. If you're in your twenties or early thirties, retirement is almost certainly something of an abstract issue to you. You reckon you've still got plenty of time left to work it out and put away what you need to make your later life comfortable.

If you're in your late thirties or forties, however, the idea of retirement is starting to loom larger. In 20 years or so you will be approaching 60 or 65. At about the same time that you are beginning to head towards retirement, your child will be entering further education. How are you going to pull both of those off at the same time?

Obviously the same basic rule applies here as in saving for university – get started as early as you can. And even if you are starting late, and it doesn't seem like much, keep at it. Having something set aside, no matter how little, is better than having nothing.

The best gift you can give your children when you are older is to be financially secure. You and your partner want to be able to take care of yourselves, and this means having adequate resources in retirement. The last thing you want in your old age is to be a burden on your children. Getting a head start on planning and saving for these things will put you in a stronger position over the long run.

Job, Work, Career

Becoming a father produces many changes in your life. But one thing does not change: your need to generate income to support yourself and your family. In this chapter you learn how fatherhood can affect your job and career, how to approach your employer about taking time off when the baby comes, and other work-related issues.

Your Role as Provider

Much of the advice given to new fathers and fathers-to-be comes from females and has (naturally) a female point of view. It tends to focus on the nurturing aspects of a father's role – being an emotional support for your partner, being there for her during childbirth and assisting her around the house and pitching in to help with the baby. These are important and useful tasks, but they do not encompass the entire universe of what a man needs to think about and do when he is about to become a father. A father's most fundamental job is to provide for his family.

The woman is in a vulnerable position during pregnancy. At some point as she nears full term, she will no longer be able to work at a job. After birth there will also be a time in which she cannot work and must tend to the baby's as well as her own needs. As a father, you must help create a safe and protected place for the mother and baby to be.

In the majority of families, the responsibility of being the primary income-earner still falls on the shoulders of the man. And most fathers are happy to have it. They see and know how much their partner is doing, and want to carry their share of the load. Contributing to their family by working is a powerful way to do that.

One 1998 survey of working fathers showed that they spend close to four hours a day with their children, an increase from less than three hours a day in 1965. In contrast, mothers today spend five and a half hours a day with their children. Despite the huge influx of women into the workplace, mothers spent about the same amount of time with their children in 1965.

Planning for When the Baby Comes

When you have a baby, there are lots of variables to consider in terms of your work and your partner's work. But one thing is certain. Unless you are independently wealthy, you need to keep the money rolling in. What this means in practical terms is that you need to keep your job or business going during the pregnancy and after the baby comes. That is, in a nutshell, the challenge of modern parenthood – balancing the needs of work and family.

Both fathers and mothers face this challenge together. While the man may make more money than his partner, that does not necessarily mean that his income alone can pay all the bills. The old paradigm – man as sole breadwinner, woman as homemaker – is becoming rarer and rarer in today's economic climate. The cost of living in some parts of the country is simply too high for families to make it on one income. Both parents must work.

Questions in Search of Answers

The most immediate impact on your financial situation is the temporary loss of your partner's income. She is going to have to leave work in the eighth or ninth month – and if you are having twins, it may be much sooner than that. Then she will need to stay home with the baby for at least a month to six weeks, and possibly longer, depending on her job situation and your finances.

Here is a question that needs an answer: how long does your partner want to stay at home with the baby? Three months? Six months? Forever? You need to find out what her expectations are in this area because they will affect her job and your overall financial planning.

Here is another question that needs an answer: how long do you want to take off from work after the baby is born? Due to the demands of the job and the need to keep money coming in, you will probably have less flexibility than your partner in this regard. Most men stay at home for a week or two after the baby is born. If you want to stay at home for longer, you will need to work it out with your employer and again, do some financial planning.

Give yourself some time with your partner to talk about these issues. You cannot decide them by yourself, nor should you. What your partner wants to do after the child is born will affect you, and vice versa. Talking about money with your partner is sometimes uncomfortable and emotional, but it is necessary.

The Domino Effect

When it was just the two of you, you had more freedom on money issues. She made money and helped with the bills. But a baby in the house (or on the way) adds a new element to all financial and job-related decisions. Any action or decision by one member of the family will inevitably tip over a domino that affects the others.

Your partner, for instance, may want to leave her job after the baby comes. Or she may be willing to go back to work, but only after she has had plenty of time at home with her new child – for instance, a year. You may argue that you cannot afford for her to do that, but she may reply that raising a child is the most important thing in the world and that her baby needs her.

Talk to your partner as soon as you can. Get a sense of her wishes and expectations (although they are certainly subject to change). Well before the baby arrives, be prepared for the financial pressures that the three of you will face.

Steps to Take at Work

As we discussed in Chapter 2, every father-to-be must assess his company's work culture before he announces to his colleagues and his boss that he is going to become a father. Some companies will be supportive, but many will not. Becoming a father may make you slightly less devoted to the organization. You may be less willing (and able) to work after hours or travel for long periods away from home, and your boss may not like this.

In many cases, what happens when a man becomes a father is that he becomes more devoted to his job, not less. The reason is obvious: he needs that precious lucre. Many fathers-to-be work overtime (or take a second job) to pay off bills and build up their nest egg. Pregnancy is a good time for this because the baby has not yet arrived and your responsibilities at home are not as great as they will be after she's born.

Whatever your job, you are almost certainly not the first person in the history of your organization to become a parent. Your company (and your partner's, too) has policies and procedures in place regarding these issues. It's up to you to find out what these are.

- Talk to other employees who are parents to see how they proceeded in your situation.
- Review your employee manual (if your organization has one) to see what your rights and responsibilities are.
- Talk to the human resources or personnel department to make sure you understand the company's procedures and policies.
- Talk to your supervisor or boss about your plans.

The more informed you are, the better off you and your partner will be. Policies about leave and benefits vary widely, however, and her company may handle things differently from yours. She will need to go through the same information-gathering process at her job.

 Don't wait until the last minute to tell your employer that you are going to be a father and that you want some time off when the baby arrives. Most companies do not appreciate surprises of this kind. They need and deserve time to plan for your absence to ensure your work gets done while you're gone. For more information visit www.workingfamilies.org.uk.

Paternity Leave

The UK government has introduced a legal right to paternity leave of one week or two consecutive weeks of paid leave from work following birth or placement for adoption. Leave must be taken within 56 days of the birth (or the adopted child's placement with you). If the baby is born before its due date, leave must be taken within 56 days of the week the baby was due to be born. If you already have a contractual right to paternity leave you can use this if the terms are better than the statutory paternity leave.

Paternity Leave (Birth)

In order to be eligible you must:

· have or expect to have responsibility for the child's upbringing
· be the biological father of the child or the mother's husband or partner
· have worked continuously for your employer for 26 weeks up to the 15th week before the baby is due.

Paternity (Adoption)

In order to be eligible you must:

· have or expect to have responsibility for the upbringing of the child.
· be the second adoptive parent in a married couple where the other spouse is taking adoption leave or partner of the child's adopter
· have been continuously employed for 26 weeks up to the week in which the child's adopter is notified of being matched with the child.

In both the above, the partner is defined as a person (whether of the same or different sex) who lives with the mother or adopter in an enduring family relationship, but is not a blood relative.

If you're like most new fathers, you will want to take off at least one week after the baby arrives. Prime Minister Tony Blair created a political firestorm for himself when he announced that he was not going to take any time off from his job when his fourth child, Leo, was born in 2000. Critics lambasted him for advocating a pro-father, pro-family line and yet not practising it himself. One of the world's most powerful leaders caved in and spent the week at home with his wife bonding with their new son.

Leave can start on any day of the week but must be completed within 56 days of the actual birth or placement of the child. If the baby is born early, leave must be completed within the period from the actual date of birth up to 56 days after the expected week of birth. There is only one period of leave available even if it is a multiple birth or more than one child is placed. Paternity leave can also be taken if the baby is stillborn after 24 weeks or dies after birth.

Why Flexibility?

Flexibility at work means everything when you have a family – much more than when you don't. If your partner is at home and not working at a job, you can rely on her to do much of what needs to be done with the baby (at least when you're at work). But when your partner goes back to her job, all bets are off. You're going to have to step in and help out, and for that you will need flexibility.

The baby needs to go to the doctor. You have to drop her off at day care or pick her up. There is an emergency. Your partner has a late meeting and needs you to get the baby. Having a small child constantly demands your time and energy.

Negotiating Flexibility

Whether or not you can get much flexibility at work depends on lots of factors. First comes your employer and the nature of your work. It may be that your company absolutely needs you to be on the job from eight to five, and there's nothing you can do about it. Other companies may be willing to be more flexible on hours as long as the work still gets done. In that case, perhaps you can do some of your work at home.

Here is where being a good employee pays off. If you are a conscientious worker who has paid his dues at the company, flexibility will be easier to negotiate than if you have been perceived as demanding or negative in the past. Whatever plan you come up with to create flexibility, remember that your boss is not going to be thinking first about you but about his own situation. You must devise a plan that works for him too, or it's not going to work.

Your boss or employer must follow company policies. He or she cannot grant special privileges to you but not to other employees. That is why it sometimes helps to check things out – talk to other employees, perhaps, and know what has been done in the past– before approaching him or her.

Small Ways to Gain Flexibility

For many fathers and fathers-to-be, flexibility on the job is a luxury. They may work for a business that cannot or will not grant privileges to its employees. They may run a small business with only a few employees and simply need to be there from sunrise to sunset. Or they may work for themselves. Shutting down the business, even for a little while, means that the money stops coming in.

Still, even men with the tightest schedules imaginable can usually find ways to create some flexibility that allows them to spend more time with their family. Perhaps you can juggle your hours a little – for instance, come in at seven and leave at four. This gets you home earlier in the evening, which corresponds better with the baby's schedule and allows you to spend more time with her. Another way to create time is to take a shorter lunch break, which may enable you to leave work earlier.

Other Job Options

Everybody's work situation is different, so finding flexibility will require different solutions for different people. You and your employer may be able to agree on a more radical approach, such as squeezing your regular 40-hour week into four days, rather than the usual five – here, you go into overdrive and work four consecutive ten-hour days, giving you three full days off.

These approaches may only be practical for a short time. Eventually, your employer may need you to work your normal hours, as you always have. Until that happens, though, you have managed to get some extra time to spend at home with your newborn. Here are some other job options worth thinking about and discussing with your employer:

- *Job sharing* – dividing your duties and hours with another person to give you more free time.
- *Part-time* – reducing your regular hours of work and taking a pro rata pay cut.
- *Telecommuting* – working from home a day or two a week.
- *Sabbatical* – taking extended (unpaid) leave from the company.

Like most men, you may not be able or willing to reduce your income, even if you want to stay home more with your child. With your partner not producing income for the moment, you need to work. In essence, when you have a baby, you take on a second full-time job – fatherhood.

Her Job and Workplace

If your partner is working, she needs to go through the same steps you did at your job, finding out about her company's maternity leave policies and talking to her colleagues and boss. She may have looked into all of this as soon as she learned she was pregnant.

It is also worth talking to your partner about such issues as workplace safety and comfort. Does she stare at a computer for long hours every day? The radiation emitted by a computer monitor has thus far been shown to have no harmful effects on pregnant women or the developing life inside them. But what about the ergonomics of her chair and desk? Can she stand up and go to the bathroom as often as she needs to?

Because of the financial benefits, it is natural to want your partner to stay at work as long as possible. But she may not be up to the challenge. Encourage her to do only what she can, and no more. Reassure her that her health comes first and that money will sort itself out somehow.

Pregnant women who can sit during the day generally stay at work longer than those who must stand at work, such as on supermarket checkouts. But there is no established norm. The length of time a woman continues working depends on her and the pregnancy. If your partner has a high-risk pregnancy, her doctor may recommend complete bed rest for several weeks or more.

Gender Roles

The Equal Opportunities Commission (EOC) published some interesting research in 2002. It found that while many dads recognize the importance of 'being there' for their children, they tend to play a supporting role at home, rather than taking equal responsibility for day-to-day caring and domestic tasks. But many mothers have low expectations of what the father 'being there' actually means.

The main reasons for mums taking responsibility for childcare are the fact that women tend to earn less than their partner, and the high cost of childcare. Researchers also found that men are put off undertaking certain tasks at home (from changing nappies to cooking) by a lack of confidence and a fear they won't do it well.

Differing Views of Work

The EOC found that, where both parents work full-time, dad is more likely to say that being the main breadwinner is not important to them. He is also more likely to take on a greater level of responsibility for childcare. Many men say that fatherhood changes their attitude to work and makes them feel more responsible, but they make limited actual changes. On the other hand, most mums make major changes to their working lives. Sometimes men make changes to their job that mean they spend less time with their family as a result of pressure to be the breadwinner and support.

Mums are generally expected to make changes in working patterns and be 'on-call' for emergencies, but dads are not. Even today, few dads in the UK consider part-time or flexible working.

Earning a living is important to men. So is being able to spend time with their families. In one recent poll, more than 80 per cent of all men between the ages of 20 and 39 said that a work schedule that gives them time to spend with their family is more important than earning a high salary.

The Employer's Perspective

Many employers, says the EOC, expect work to be the main focus of a man's attention – whether or not he's a father – leaving dads little room to fit in family commitments. Some dads don't mind this and are happy to take responsibility for managing their own work–life balance; others say it causes friction between work and home.

Dads are, by and large, unaware of types of family-friendly working policies, says the EOC, or assume that family-friendly working is not intended for them. The companies in their turn don't always shout about these policies to fathers.

However, since 6 April 2003 employers have had a legal duty to consider requests for flexible working from employees who are parents of young children. To be eligible, you must have parental responsibility for a child aged under six or for a disabled child aged under 18.

You may be dissatisfied with your job. It may not pay enough or offer adequate flexibility. Even so, do not make any rash moves. You need to hang on to your job until after your child is born and probably for some months after that. It provides much-needed income.

Getting a Better Job

Generally speaking, pregnancy is not a good time to leave a job or change jobs. With your personal life heading into uncertain, perhaps rocky seas, it is best to keep a steady hand on the employment rudder. But in some situations, pregnancy may be the prompt you need to make a change in your employment situation. A baby can change your attitude towards your job or work. What may have been a perfect fit before may not be quite so ideal anymore.

Reasons for Dissatisfaction

Due to the increased financial pressures on you, the money you're making at your job may no longer cut it. Now that you have a baby at home, that two-hour commute to and from work may seem impossible. You do not want to spend your time sitting in traffic or on a train. You want to get home at a decent hour so you can do more with your boy than give him a kiss at night before he goes to bed.

You used to work regularly till six or seven at night. After the baby comes, you may find yourself slipping out of the office a few minutes before five. Your line manager may not like this. She may have come to expect long hours from you, and she's disappointed now that you seem to have developed split loyalties between the company and your family. This may cause her to give you a hard time, which makes you think about making a change.

The Need for More Education

In order to support their families and give them a better life, many fathers realize that they need to get more training or go back to college or to take employment-specific evening classes. It is possible you will find yourself in this situation. In today's rapidly changing economy, it is no exaggeration to say that the job you hold at this moment may not exist in five or ten years.

The bright side of this picture is that the changes occurring in the economy are also creating jobs and opportunities that did not exist five or ten years ago. But to take advantage of these opportunities, you may need to get a specific kind of training or a more advanced degree. You may need to leave your job or reduce your hours and take out loans and obtain financial assistance.

CHAPTER 9: JOB, WORK, CAREER

Obviously you will need to work all this out beforehand with your partner. If you're earning less money, she will probably have to take up the slack with her income. And before making any radical changes, you may want to wait until the baby is a little older. But these are the kinds of changes – leaving a job in order to go back to college to get a better job – that develop momentum when you start a family.

Working from Home

An increasing number of men today are self-employed. You may be one of them, working in your spare bedroom at home, sitting in front of the computer in your bathrobe and slippers, setting your own hours and schedule as you see fit. Because of this, you may feel pity for those 'wage slaves' who must work normal jobs where they have to worry about their company policies or what their boss thinks.

Feel smug no more. Your home office is about to be thrown into complete turmoil. Quiet and sanity and free time will all be relics of the past. Why is that, you ask? Because in the space of a few short weeks or months, you are about to be invaded.

Home Invasion

In the last weeks of her pregnancy, your partner will probably stop working. Consequently, she will spend more time at home than she has in the past. This will represent a change for you, because you are used to working alone and having the place to yourself during the day, but you will adjust. This adjustment is nothing, though, compared to the one you must make when the baby appears.

A baby does not just arrive in a house – he takes over. His needs reign supreme, and they must be satisfied instantly. Otherwise tears will stream down his cute chubby cheeks and his cries will pierce your eardrums like a heavy metal vocal. Even when his needs are filled, he still cries. As his father, there is nothing for you to do but feed him and change him and walk him and burp him and pray that he falls asleep at some point to give you a break.

Unemployed fathers have no reason to feel bad about themselves. If you happen to be out of work, you can still be a loving, hands-on presence for your partner and your child (when she arrives). Your baby does not care how much money you make, only that you are there for her.

Finding a Quiet Space Outside the Home

But you still have to work, right? Even if you keep the door to your office closed at all times – good grief, even if you soundproof the door and the walls – it is going to be a challenging work environment. You will hear the baby's cries, as well as the tired desperation in your partner's voice, and inevitably you will open the door and offer to help. Your partner may not wait for you to offer – she may bang on the door and demand it. In any event, when you work at home with a new baby, expect to help out. A lot.

During the pregnancy, it might be wise to check out other possible workplace options than your own home. Can you do some of your work at a library? What about temporarily borrowing or renting a room at a friend's or neighbour's house? If these are not practical, you may want to investigate the possibility of renting an office for six months to a year to get a quiet space to work.

You can also anticipate that you will be working unusual hours in the first months after the baby comes home. You will need to take care of the baby to give your partner a break and let her sleep, and your partner will need to watch him while you work and sleep.

Flexibility is the key when you have a child, whether you work at home, at a job, or whether you run your own business. Advance planning is also useful. Find out how much paid leave you and your wife can take. Talk to your employer, who may be sympathetic to you and willing to arrange a routine that works for you both. Thinking ahead may help you to get the routine you would like.

Chapter 10

Health: Yours, Hers and the Baby's

Your number-one concern as a father is the health and well-being of your partner and the child on the way. But while you – and the doctors and everyone else – are paying so much attention to them, don't forget another important person: yourself. Here are some tips on keeping a sound body and mind while being an expectant father.

Leading the Way

One of the issues that regularly pops up in discussions about sports today is whether or not professional sportsmen and sportswomen are role models. Whether you think these professionals are role models or not, a child's most influential role models are her father and mother. Babies and children are like little sponges, mimicking the habits and behaviour of the people who are around them the most. A child first learns from his parents and siblings, while the other influences on her life – television, school, peers – come later.

This realization will hit home to you most powerfully at some point after the baby is born. She will be crying or making a noise about something – and you will hear a familiar inflection in her voice. Or she will wrinkle her nose or move her hands in a certain way, and you will think, 'Hey, that's me. That is what I do.' You were not consciously teaching her how to do this, and yet she picked it up by watching you and being around you.

Alcohol

The realization that you can have such a profound impact on another human being can be humbling for many men. It is one reason why some have trouble making the adjustment to fatherhood. 'Hey, I can barely take care of myself', they say to themselves, 'and now I'm supposed to take care of a kid? I don't think so.'

Although your partner is a mature adult, capable of acting and making decisions on her own, what you do can have a big impact on her too. You are not her role model in the same way that you will be for your child. But your behaviour can influence hers in both negative and positive ways.

Alcohol's Effect on the Developing Foetus

Not everything is known about what effect alcohol has on the baby inside, but we know this: too much is bad. Pregnant women who drink too much can cause foetal alcohol syndrome, which produces physical and mental disabilities in the child. Even moderate amounts of alcohol consumption may cause miscarriages, undernourished babies and learning difficulties. For these and other reasons, doctors strongly recommend that women stop drinking alcohol while they are pregnant.

Now, your wife's obstetrician may privately tell her that a glass of wine or lager every now and then won't hurt anybody. In fact, pregnant women themselves say they occasionally need half a glass of Chardonnay to relax. But only occasionally, and definitely no hard alcohol – no gin and tonics or rum and Cokes!

Your Role

'OK, so my partner has to stop drinking', you may be thinking at this point, 'what does this have to do with me?' Common sense will tell you that if you're knocking back a beer and a couple of glasses of wine night after night, it is going to be harder for your partner to stay away from the alcohol. There will obviously be alcohol around the house, and that means there is more temptation for her to pour herself a glass of something when she's feeling down.

If you drink, you might consider stopping during your partner's pregnancy. If you want to continue, cut down on how much you drink. Have a few beers with your friends after work, but don't bring any alcohol home. Your resolve to cut down or even stop will be viewed positively by your partner as another sign of support and togetherness for her.

Different couples work it out in different ways. One mother-to-be was concerned about her partner's heavy drinking and wanted him to stop, but he refused. One night they went out together, and when he ordered his usual – double Scotch on the rocks and a beer – she did the same. When he drank his, she drank hers.

'If you insist on getting drunk again', she told him, 'so will I.' And even though she was five months pregnant, she meant it. His drinking, if he kept at it, was potentially going to harm their child and destroy their relationship. He got the message, and it scared him to death. Eventually he gave up drinking – not just during the pregnancy, but for good.

Cigarette Smoking

Smoking cigarettes is one of the worst health hazards of pregnancy. Pregnant women are urged to stop because the smoke they inhale does not just go into their lungs – the baby gets an unhealthy dose of it too. A mother's smoking can cause mammoth problems for the child, such as developmental disabilities and disorders, pregnancy complications, premature birth and even death.

That's the bad news, but there is good news. Evidence to date shows that even if a woman has smoked all her life, as long as she does not do so during pregnancy, her child will not be harmed. A mother-to-be needs to put away the cigarettes as soon as she learns that she's pregnant.

If your pregnant partner smokes, she is at greater risk of having a low-birthweight baby. Babies born to women who smoke when pregnant are, by and large, almost half a pound lighter than those of women who don't smoke – and low birthweight babies are more susceptible to illness, disability and even death. Smoking may have other harmful effects, too, including miscarriage, problems with the placenta, vaginal bleeding and premature delivery. It also trebles the risk of cot death.

Finding the Motivation

Mark Twain said that stopping smoking was the easiest thing in the world; he had done it 30 or 40 times. Most smokers would heartily agree. People may know intellectually that it is bad for them and they need to stop, but how do you actually do it?

Under ordinary circumstances, it is hard sometimes to find the motivation to stop smoking (or drinking alcohol). But when you are about to become a parent, motivation is no longer in short supply. You know exactly what you need to do, and why, and suddenly it no longer seems impossible.

Once More, with Feeling

If your partner smokes and is pregnant, it is best for her to stop smoking. She may be the most motivated and determined person in the world, but stopping anything cold turkey is hard for anyone. Once again, she is going to need your help.

If you smoke, it is going to make it that much harder for her to stop or cut back. When she sees you smoking, that will make her want to light up, too. Then there is the issue of secondhand smoke. Having your pregnant partner breathing the smoke from your cigarettes may harm the life inside her. Even if you take it outside or try not to do it in her presence, she is still going to smell it on your breath and clothes.

As with the restrictions on drinking, you may view this as punitive: 'She's the one who's pregnant. Why do I have to suffer too?' Another way to look at it is that stopping is something the two of you can do together. While she's pregnant, make a pact and agree to throw away the cigarettes and keep them out of the house. Doing it as a couple – with each person trying not to disappoint the other – may give you further motivation and determination. Nobody's perfect. If your partner, in a moment of weakness, breaks down and has a cigarette, it is not the end of the world. Just encourage her to stop at one and get back on her healthy track. A forgiving approach reaps better results than a critical, judgmental one.

If your partner needs help to give up smoking, encourage her to talk to her midwife: there may be a local support scheme for people trying to quit. Or persuade her to ring the NHS 'Smoking in Pregnancy' helpline – 0800 169 9169 – a special service geared to the needs and concerns of pregnant women. It's free and confidential, and the trained counsellors know how hard it is to quit, and offer support and advice. Or you could both go online and visit www.quit.org.uk.

Recreational and Over-the-Counter Drugs

Recreational drugs – such as marijuana, cocaine or ecstasy – come into the same category as cigarettes and alcohol. They are bad news. They can do damage to the baby in the womb, producing birth defects and other maladies that can affect him for his entire life.

Some people would argue that marijuana should not be lumped with cocaine and other illegal drugs, saying that it is less harmful and more benign to its users. As with cigarettes, past marijuana use does not appear to affect a developing foetus. But, again, like cigarettes, smoking pot while pregnant is a different story. The smoke your partner inhales affects the placenta, which serves as the baby's protective cocoon. Marijuana should be avoided during pregnancy, just like any other drug.

A good person to talk to about all of this is an obstetrician. Your partner may have initially had concerns that the alcohol she drank before she learned she was pregnant hurt her child. Her obstetrician no doubt assured her that this was not the case. But once a woman learns she is pregnant, she has to start acting with another person in mind, namely her baby.

For this reason, your partner also needs to speak to her doctor about any over-the-counter drugs or antibiotics she is currently taking or plans to take. Any kind of over-the-counter medication, even aspirin, may create harmful side effects for the baby. In matters of health, when you are dealing with pregnancy, follow a simple rule. Err on the side of caution. Be aware of the possible risks of any drug before taking it.

Eating Healthily

Quit drinking. Stop smoking. Cut out the illegal drugs. While each of these has positive health benefits, they might also be perceived as negatives in that you must cease and desist from activities that you were doing before your partner became pregnant and that you both considered, well, fun. For you to stop doing these things requires sacrifice.

Less of a negative and more of a positive is the idea of eating healthily. Unless you're a junk food junkie, this requires less sacrifice. And for your pregnant partner and that baby *in utero*, the benefits of a nutrition-packed diet are profound. It might even benefit you, too.

Foods to Avoid

There are some foods your pregnant partner needs to avoid, including:

· raw seafood, such as oysters or uncooked sushi.

· soft cheeses with a white rind, such as Brie and Camembert, and blue-veined cheeses like Stilton.

· paté, raw or undercooked meat, poultry and eggs (cook all meat until there are no pink bits left and eggs till they are hard). All are possible sources of bacteria that can harm your unborn child.

· liver and liver products (paté, liver sausage). They are rich in vitamin A, too much of which is bad for the developing baby.

If you're on kitchen duty, and you chopped up the chicken or fish for dinner, make sure to clean the knife and the cutting board before using them again to chop the vegetables.

If you or your partner (or any of your other children if you have any) have a history of allergies such as hay fever, asthma or eczema, then avoiding peanuts and foods that contain them during pregnancy and breastfeeding may reduce your baby's chances of developing an allergy to peanuts (a potentially life-threatening condition).

Coffee and Tea

You can breathe a sigh of relief on this one. Your partner (and by association, you) is not going to be asked to give up her morning cup of tea or coffee.

Coffee and tea with caffeine are relatively benign in their effects and have not yet been placed by medical authorities on the banned substances list. There is a difference between heavy and light caffeine consumption, however, and your partner needs to practise moderation. She may want to switch to decaffeinated coffee or herbal teas during this period.

Studies indicate that it appears to be safe for a pregnant woman to drink as many as two to three cups of coffee a day. But the higher the consumption, the more the risk apparently grows. The miscarriage rate climbs slightly for pregnant women whose coffee intake is five to six cups a day. The effects of caffeine on pregnancy are still being studied.

Remember that colas, chocolate and other substances contain caffeine. Too much caffeine can affect a person's mood and may make your partner's emotional ups and downs even more pronounced than they already are. If she's on a coffee high, she may push herself when her body really needs rest. Drinking a rich coffeehouse brew may give her an artificial feeling of fullness, causing her not to eat more wholesome foods.

Developing Healthy Habits

By now, you have noticed a clear trend in this whole pregnancy deal – the burden of just about everything falls more heavily on the woman. She is the one who must stop smoking, abstain from drinking, not take cough syrup without first calling the doctor, and cut out those mocha frappucinos from Starbucks.

And you? Well, your participation in her abstinence is optional. You have the freedom to decide whether to go along with all of this for the simple reason that your choices do not matter as much to the baby's health. You could drink like a fish and smoke unfiltered cigarettes until your lungs collapsed, and still you would not directly affect the baby.

However, you can choose to acknowledge that what you do does make a difference. You can definitely make a positive contribution to your partner's pregnancy and the developing life of your child through the choices you make. Your support and encouragement will help her make these sometimes hard sacrifices. Besides the things that have already been discussed in this chapter, here are some things she needs to do and that you can help her with:

Take her pregnancy vitamins every day
· Drink lots of fluids.
· Drink milk, or eat other calcium-rich foods such as yogurt or cottage cheese.
· Eat a variety of fruits, vegetables and wholegrain foods.
· Get plenty of protein in her diet.
· Cut down on her fat intake.
· Exercise lightly on a regular basis.
· Get plenty of rest.

Your partner has probably worked out much of this already. If she is like many first-time mothers, she's been reading the pregnancy books like mad and talking to her doctor and everybody else who has been through it to learn all she can. But your active, engaged presence in what she is going through will be a boon to her. And in the end it will help you feel more connected to your child.

What if I feel intimidated by the pregnancy?
Many men do. Partly this is because they have never experienced anything like this before, and they know nothing about it. Of course, your partner didn't either until she got pregnant. The more involved you become, the less intimidated you will feel.

Cooking

Every couple has its own kitchen culture. With some couples, the man does most of the cooking. With others, the man and the woman share the job. Some couples work it out along more traditional lines, with the woman doing most of the cooking.

Almost invariably, when a woman becomes pregnant, the man must learn to take on a greater role in the food preparation and shopping. Particularly early in the pregnancy, when the woman is suffering from morning sickness, she may not feel like cooking or eating anything, so if a father-to-be wants something to eat, he is probably going to have to get on with it and do it himself.

The Joy of Cooking

Men who are used to having their partners cook for them may resent this change of roles. They may prefer the old system – she cooks, he washes up – and decide to simply make do as best they can until their partner feels good enough to get back into the kitchen again.

For other fathers-to-be, pregnancy may present them with an unexpected opportunity. Suddenly thrust into the kitchen, they may find they actually like cooking and get into it.

Stick to the Basics

The first thing to know about cooking, if you are a novice, is that you do not need to prepare a masterpiece to impress your partner. You may remember from your bachelor days that a woman will appreciate almost anything you prepare because it means she doesn't have to make a meal herself. And it shows you are trying. Your pregnant partner may appreciate this most of all.

One essential element of good cooking is using fresh ingredients. Whatever meal you choose to make – roast chicken with green beans, spaghetti Bolognese with a tossed green salad, chicken burritos and guacamole dip – will taste better if you avoid frozen or tinned vegetables and rely on fresh. Green leafy vegetables and fruits are a rich source of vitamin C, iron, calcium and other good minerals, all of which your partner needs (as do you).

Consult a Cookbook

The joke about men is that when driving a car, they refuse to ask for directions. They would rather drive around in circles than stoop to the indignity of asking a stranger to straighten them out. This may be true of some men in the kitchen as well. They regard cookbooks much the way John Belushi's Blutarski in *Animal House* looked askance at textbooks and refused to open one.

Cookbooks contain recipes and show basic techniques. They tell you how long your beef stew – protein is vital for pregnant women, and meat is a prime source for it – should stay in the oven and at what temperature. There are cookbooks targeted especially at men, and many supermarkets have free recipe cards.

When cooking for a pregnant woman, you may need to go easy on spicy or hot foods. More exotic cuisines, such as Indian or Thai, may not sit well in her stomach. This doesn't mean that you and she have to give up curry – just go easy on the chilli!

Exercise

The benefits of exercise for pregnant women are as clear and strong as the benefits of eating well. Exercise can help her stand up straighter, improve her blood circulation and possibly relieve constipation, give her a better night's sleep and give her a boost in energy. Exercise can give her a mental break too, taking her mind off the pregnancy for a while.

The need for your partner to engage in moderate exercise may produce an unintended benefit for you as well. You may be willing to put down the remote, get off the sofa and take a walk or bike ride with her. While she gains weight, you may be inspired to lose some.

Your partner should talk to her midwife before she starts exercising. Skiing, horse riding and other sports in which she could potentially fall and hurt herself and the baby are off-limits. Nor can she lift weights. Her midwife will be able to give her guidelines on safe activities.

Now you may not be a couch potato. On the contrary, you may be a total gym fiend or a triathlete. Your first thought may be, 'Me? Exercise with a pregnant woman? You must be joking.'

Like so many of the other activities discussed in this chapter, your partner will be more inclined to exercise if you go with her. The downside for you, it is true, is that you may have to slow down a little (or a lot) due to her condition. Here are a few suggestions on what you can do together:

- Walking or light jogging
- Swimming
- Friendly game of tennis
- Golf (probably with a buggy)
- Cycling
- Table tennis
- Badminton
- Light yoga or stretching

Exercise will help your partner feel and look better. It will be equally beneficial for you. And you'll get these benefits at the same time that you and your partner are engaged in a shared activity, thus promoting togetherness as a couple. Regular moderate exercise may promote another aspect of your life as well – your sex life.

Her Need for Rest

Virtually from the beginning of her pregnancy, your partner has been tired. So tired, in fact, she almost seems like a different person. Even on her good days, she seems to have little energy. This affects everything. You ask her to go on a walk with you, but she doesn't feel up to it. You put on your chef's hat and whip up a masterpiece in the kitchen, but she is too tired (or sick) to eat much of it. Worse still, she never feels like going out anymore. Most nights, all she wants to do is sleep.

Such is life with a pregnant woman. She may have periods of high energy – particularly in the second trimester – but even then she complains about how tired she is. Her tiredness may be a drag from your point of view. It is essential to realize, though, that rest is critical. She is sleeping for herself as well as for that life growing inside her.

The primary goal of all pregnant couples is simple: healthy baby, healthy mother. Your partner can go a long way to achieve this by quitting or cutting down on drinking and cigarette smoking, stopping recreational drug use, watching her caffeine intake, eating the right foods, exercising moderately, and getting lots of rest. And you can help her do it all.

Chapter 11

Sex During Pregnancy

Sex during pregnancy is not one of those oxymorons like 'jumbo prawn' or 'working holiday'. Sex during pregnancy does indeed exist, and many couples report that it can be quite rewarding. This chapter explains how to get the most from your sex life while moving towards greater intimacy with your partner.

Sex and the Pregnant Father

Pregnancy marks a new phase in your sexual relationship with your partner. The two of you have produced a child – another human being in the making. This simple yet breathtaking development has triggered a series of changes in your life, including your sex life.

When you were single, your sex life may have been an active one. You may have gone out with a variety of women and had longer relationships with some of them. Or maybe you went out with only a select few. Out of all your prior experiences came the luckiest one: your partner, the mother of your child.

When you went from being strictly single to a man in a committed relationship, your sex life inevitably changed. In the beginning, the infatuation you felt for your partner produced frequent sparks in the bedroom. Over the years you may have found that these sparks, while still white-hot in intensity, occur less frequently. Every couple's sexual relationship changes and becomes different as their feelings for each other mature.

Now you are entering a period of uncertainty and perhaps even confusion. Your partner's body is changing along with, perhaps, her libido. You're not sure what it all means – for now or in the future. But in every phase in your past sex life, you have had to grow and adjust to changing circumstances. This one is no different.

Understanding Your Partner

It is worthwhile to note that your partner is likely to be experiencing many of the same emotions that you are – perhaps to an even greater degree. She has never been through any of this before, either. The physical and emotional changes she is experiencing, while giving her immense joy on one level, may fill her with doubts. She may also wonder what all this means to the two of you as a couple.

She may worry about your feelings for her at this time. Do you still find her attractive? Does she still turn you on?

One study found that after about the third month, 10 per cent of all pregnant couples were not having sex. By the ninth month, the number of abstaining couples had risen to 33 per cent. However, in this same study, about 40 per cent of all the couples surveyed were still having and enjoying sex into the ninth month.

What Stage Is She In?

The key to sex during pregnancy is understanding the stage your partner is in and adjusting to it. The term of pregnancy consists of three trimesters of roughly three months apiece. Each trimester represents a stage in the baby's development that produces corresponding changes in your partner's physical growth and emotional moods.

The first trimester is when morning sickness is most likely to occur. Because your partner may frequently feel nauseated and tired, her desire for sex may be somewhat limited. The last trimester is the final three months before birth occurs. This is when your partner's body grows to its biggest proportions. Feeling heavy and (as always) tired, she may not exactly feel like a sex kitten at this time either.

Every woman and every woman's pregnancy are different. But, generally speaking, the best time for sexual relations for pregnant couples is in the second trimester – from months four to six. Your partner's morning sickness has passed, and yet her body has not grown ungainly. Her hormones may have imbued her with that famous pregnancy 'glow', when everything about her radiates with reborn energy. These surging feelings of health and wellness may translate into a renewed interest in bedroom activities.

Tuning into Her

A man's body is, in the sexual sphere, obviously far different from that of a woman. Men do not menstruate, and their moods do not rise and fall during the month because of this. Although a woman stops menstruating during pregnancy, her moods are still connected to the rhythms of her body.

Because of the physical changes she is experiencing, her libido may have decreased. She may simply not be as interested in sex as she was before. It's nobody's fault; it's just the way it is. Then again, there may be instances in the second trimester or at other times during the pregnancy when she is just as randy for you as she was when you first started sleeping together. It is up to you to assess her mood in terms of sex and act accordingly.

If your partner seems uninterested in sex, don't take it personally. It is not because she suddenly finds you less attractive or somehow less of a man. Don't blame her, either. Her feelings about sex are being shaped to a large degree by the hormonal changes occurring inside her body.

Your Attitude

When they offer suggestions about sex, most pregnancy manuals advise men to tune into what their partners are feeling. Be sensitive to her moods and her situation at that moment, they say. This is good advice, but what these manuals never seem to acknowledge is that the man may be experiencing a variety of his own feelings, too.

Many men get turned on by pregnancy and their partner's pregnant body. Creating a child is a happy affirmation of their masculinity. Other men are not so sure about the whole business. Their feelings are more complicated, perhaps even troubled to some extent. These feelings may affect their view of sex during pregnancy and their relationship with their partner.

Your View of Her Body

It's all right to admit it (at least to yourself) – you may not be entirely sold on what your partner looks like at this moment. This may have temporarily decreased your desire for her. And a tiny voice in the back of your head may be wondering if this is going to turn into a permanent condition – you being less interested in her sexually, and at the same time she being less interested in you.

Some fathers-to-be, however, do not mind the extra weight on their partners; they love it, in fact. As a pregnant woman gets closer to delivering, her breasts begin to lactate. The father-to-be can taste the sweetness of mother's milk even before his child does.

Attitude is everything. If you are put off initially by your partner's changing body shape, try to take a different attitude about it. Relax. Accept it for what it is, and know that it is temporary. If she senses you being distant or critical, she may in turn withdraw from you physically, and this will affect your togetherness as a couple.

Your Partner as a Mother

Your partner may be thrilled at the prospects of becoming a mother. However, your view of this new development may be somewhat different. While you may know that your partner is going to be a sensational parent, she is nevertheless taking on a new role. No longer merely your partner, she is becoming your child's mother as well.

Sexually speaking, this may give you pause. You may never have made love to somebody's mother before, certainly not the mother of your own child. A thought like that can get into your head and play games with sexual desire, if you let it.

Your feelings about your partner may be complicated by your feelings about your own mother and her relationship with your father. Your father may have been an outsider in his own home, a man who could often be found out in the shed because that was where he was most comfortable. Perhaps this was partly his own predilection, but it could also have been the result of your mother's shutting him out of the life of the family. Could this happen to you too?

Trust in Time

Some of the changes you are experiencing with your partner may, in fact, be more or less permanent. After she gives birth, she may not lose all the weight she gained during the pregnancy. Even if she loses the weight, the chances are that her shape, particularly her breasts and hips, will be different. You may have no other choice but to learn to live with the new contours of her body.

It will take time for the great physical thing the two of you had before pregnancy to return. Her body will need to physically heal after giving birth. It sometimes takes months before the two of you can comfortably have sex again. Even when it becomes physically OK for her, her mind may be on the baby and her own issues and not on you. You may not receive much satisfaction. Beyond that, you may wonder if she isn't into sex any more for some reason that has something to do with you.

But things could go the other way, too. She may lose a few pounds. Her sexual desire (as well as yours) may return to normal. What you two had together in the bedroom may come back better than before. All these things can happen, but they will take time.

How do you approach your partner for sex during this time?
Ask her. Talk to her. She may be grateful for the chance to confide what she is feeling. Your openness to her may lead her to feel more open to you and a warmer, more relaxed atmosphere for you both.

Will Sex Hurt the Baby?

This is often one of the first concerns of both men and women after they learn they are pregnant. Will sex hurt the baby, possibly causing a miscarriage or other problems? In almost every case in a normal pregnancy, the answer is no. Both of you can feel relaxed about having sex. It will not affect the child, who is well protected inside the womb.

Doctors and other experts on pregnancy encourage couples to continue having normal sexual relations – if they feel up to it. You may be parents-to-be now, but you are still a functioning couple. A vital aspect of a good relationship is healthy sexual relations. Although your partner's sex drive, in particular, will go up and down during the pregnancy, with patience and understanding, this is no reason to stop doing it.

For couples in high-risk pregnancies, or in cases where the woman has a history of early miscarriages, sexual intercourse may be restricted, at least for the first 14 weeks. Talk to your doctor or midwife. Even in these situations, however, it may be possible for one partner to pleasure the other without having intercourse.

These sorts of sexual anxieties are common among pregnant couples. Some feel these things deeply, while some only think about them in passing. Some other common worries about intercourse during this time include the following:

·   The foetus is somehow aware of its parents having sex.
·   When it penetrates the vagina, the penis will puncture the amniotic sac.
·   Having sex early in a normal pregnancy will stimulate a woman to go into premature labour.
·   Having sex in the ninth month of a normal pregnancy will cause a woman to go into labour.
·   The penis may penetrate so deeply it will touch the head of the baby.

Most of your worries, although common, are unfounded. Talk to a doctor or midwife if you have concerns about sex, even if these concerns seem trivial or embarrassing. One thing you do not have to worry about, however, is your partner's getting pregnant while she is still pregnant. This is one long-held belief that is absolutely true. With no need to worry about birth control for the moment, both the man and woman often feel sexually free for the first time in a long while. This can allow them to open up and really enjoy sex.

For most of the pregnancy, the mother and child are protected from infection as long as the man does not have a sexually transmittable disease. But in the ninth month, the amniotic sac that holds the baby could rupture at any time, exposing him to potentially harmful organisms. Some experts recommend using a condom in the final one to two months of pregnancy.

Holding and Cuddling

When making love, men tend to focus on doing the deed – sexual intercourse. Women tend to prefer foreplay – the things that lead up to doing the deed. When your partner becomes pregnant, if you are truly interested in arousing her sexually, you will need to focus even more heavily on foreplay.

For some men, this is a joy and a blessing, not a curse. They are turned on by the full-figured shape of their pregnant partner and are happy to oblige her. However, for other men, foreplay may be seen as more of a chore.

What Women Are Feeling

There are many reasons that pregnant women cannot jump into bed and instantly start making mad passionate love. For one thing, they cannot jump. Depending how far along they are in the pregnancy, even walking may be uncomfortable for them. For another, they are often bone-tired. All they want to do in bed is sleep.

A pregnant woman often does not feel at ease in her body. Her back hurts, her feet hurt and her whole body is a bundle of small and not-so-small aches and pains. Later in the pregnancy, she may experience some vaginal discomfort with penetration. All of this may have made her less interested in sex – and may have turned her off it altogether.

Take It Easy

The best lovemaking approach for a pregnant woman is to simply hold her and touch her in a non-sexual way at first. Cuddle with her in bed. Rub her back and shoulders. Run your fingers along her skin and belly. Avoid touching, as long as you can, her breasts and vaginal area.

Want to give a gift to your partner? Give her a foot massage. Even if the rest of her body is uncomfortable, she will almost certainly respond to gentle rubbing of her feet. Your technique is less important than the fact that you are willing to do it, and she will appreciate this fact.

Your partner's nipples and breasts may be especially sensitive during this time. This can be a good thing, because her sensations in these areas may be more intense than normal. Be gentle, go slow and tune in to her responses.

Feeling the Baby Kick

Around the sixth month or so, and frequently before then, you can feel your baby kick by placing your hand on your partner's abdomen. She will show you where to put your hand based on where she is feeling the kick. This is another unique chance for bedroom intimacy, shared only by couples who are pregnant.

When the mother is active, the child inside her tends to be quiet. When the mother lies down at the end of the day to rest, that is when the child generally starts bouncing around and kicking. Some nights or mornings, though, he may be resting and still. At that time, you may want to sing or talk to him. Placing your mouth close to your partner's belly and singing to it may seem like the craziest thing in the world, but it will increase your feelings of connection, not only with your child, but with his mother as well.

Finding a Comfortable Position

The comfortable and enjoyable position you find for sex will change, depending on how far along the pregnancy is. In the early stages, you can be on top of your partner. As she gets bigger and bigger, this will be less and less comfortable for you both. You may continue to be on top of her for a while if you hold yourself above her with your arms like you're doing a push-up. But eventually this will not work any more, and you will have to stop using this position.

The reverse – her on top, you on the bottom – may also work well. This gives her a little more control, which may help her relax. And your body weight won't be pressing against her stomach.

You may find, as the pregnancy develops, that you are sharing your bed with pillows that your partner is using to make herself comfortable. These pillows come in a variety of shapes: wedges to support her growing belly, cylinders for her neck, and other types of pillows that may make your side of the bed slightly smaller. She can use these pillows to help her get into a comfortable position. If she is comfortable and enjoying herself, and you are doing the same, you know you are doing something right.

Variations to Try

Another popular position for pregnant couples is doggie-style, as it is known. The woman is on her hands and knees, supporting her abdomen with pillows. You can get behind her and enter her vaginally. But again, as the months go by and she gets bigger, she may grow less comfortable with this position.

A popular pregnancy position in the later months is spooning. This is when a couple lies on their sides in bed, the man behind the woman. Spooning is effective because her body is completely supported by the bed. She may place one of those crazy pillows she has between her knees to get more comfortable.

Touching and Oral Sex

Of course, there are ways to satisfy your partner and yourself without having intercourse. This is, of course, true for pregnant couples as well. You can simulate intercourse between her thighs or breasts, with no vaginal penetration.

Your partner may feel physical discomfort during sex. This discomfort may be caused by a variety of reasons. She needs to listen to her body so she can let you in on how she's feeling, and you need to listen to what she says. You may need to pause or stop in the middle of things because she doesn't feel right.

Oral sex is another option. Cunnilingus – stimulating the woman's genitalia with your mouth and tongue – is safe as long as you do not blow any air into her vagina; doing this could cause an obstruction in a blood vessel and be dangerous for both mother and child. Fellatio – her mouth on your penis – is always safe and frequently rewarding. Masturbation is yet another alternative to intercourse.

Towards a New Intimacy

Having a child can create friction. Almost immediately, your relations with your partner began to change when she became pregnant. Your sex life is one of the biggest areas of change, possibly making life between the sheets less secure and more challenging.

Amidst these challenges, opportunities exist – opportunities for greater intimacy between you and your partner. It may sound trite, but it's true – the two of you now share something you did not before. It is not a thing at all, of course; it is your child, another human being. This bond may lead you both to find a deeper level of commitment, physically and emotionally, in your relationship.

Your sexual activities may not be as frequent or as active as they were before your partner became pregnant. As your partner's body continues to change, these changes may dampen her sex drive and make the act of intercourse uncomfortable for her. You may also secretly worry about having sex with her at this time. But taking your time and finding comfortable positions can ease your anxieties and help make sex during pregnancy a pleasurable experience for you both.

Chapter 12

Making Sound Decisions

When you first learn you are going to be a father, you have nine months or so to get your act together and prepare to have a baby. In that time, you will face a number of important issues with your partner. This chapter discusses some of these issues and how to work together to make the decisions that are right for you.

Speak Up: It's Your Child, Too

Most men have no problem making their opinion known and heard. Ask them who they think is going to win the FA Cup or the Six Nations, and they'll tell you in no uncertain terms. And if you happen to disagree with their point of view, they will tell you straight out how wrong you are.

But when the subject turns to babies, these same loud-mouthed, bull-headed lads sometimes turn into pussycats. They more or less follow what their partner says and express no opinion themselves because they feel that this whole baby business is, well, a woman's thing. To some extent this is understandable. Virtually all of the action is occurring inside your partner's body, not yours. So how are you supposed to know what to do?

Some of this timidity among men may also stem from how they were brought up. It may have been that their mother ran the house, made all the decisions, and was the dominant force in the family. Meanwhile, their father was working at his job and not around the house that much, and was perhaps not all that interested in what was going on anyway. Based on these role models, some fathers-to-be may reckon that they, too, are supposed to step back and let their partner run the show.

One of the problems with this approach is that there are lots of decisions that need to be made when you have a baby. Your partner can indeed decide some of the minor ones with little input from you. But many of the decisions being made are huge. They are going to affect not just your partner's or your baby's life, but your life, too. You can sit on the sidelines and say nothing, or you can have a voice in these decisions. Regardless of how fathers handled it in the past, most fathers today choose to speak up.

Even if your partner doesn't say so directly, she needs your input on the many decisions you both are facing. Two heads are better than one. In discussing an issue together, sometimes you can come up with an idea or answer that neither of you had thought of before.

Naming the Little One

Almost unfailingly, every parent-to-be will have an opinion on what they want to name their child. Virtually no one, male or female, stays quiet on this issue. It's too big, too important.

Names are a big issue. You realize that you are making a decision that will affect your child for the rest of his life. Wherever he goes, whatever he does, he is going to carry his name around with him. It will influence how he views himself and how others view him. Finding the right name for your child is fun, exciting and a little humbling, too.

Some Things to Consider

The name you choose for your child will in some way reflect your values as parents. Scary thought, eh? Once upon a time you may have considered yourself a free and unencumbered happy-go-lucky chap who didn't have to worry about such a boring and staid concept as 'values'. But times have changed, and now you are about to affix a name to another human being. There are many things to consider as you do this. What do you want the name to do:

- Be a reflection of your family or ethnic heritage?
- Honour a certain family member or person?
- Be similar to your own name?
- Be relatively common or something out of the ordinary?
- Be a traditional or unusual spelling?
- Be easy for other people to pronounce and spell?
- Be a name that other children won't tease him about when he gets older?

Some parents happen to hear a name and like it and decide to use it. Others refer to books to come up with ideas. Still others may have had a name in mind since they were young, knowing that if they ever had a girl, Emily is what they'd like to name her. Some couples wait to see the baby before making a final decision on a name. Whatever name you choose, it will always reflect your values and beliefs.

Surveys are held regularly to determine the most common children's names in the UK. In 2004, according to the Office for National Statistics (England and Wales only) the five most popular girls' names were 1) Emily; 2) Ellie; 3) Jessica; 4) Sophie; and 5) Chloe. The five most popular boys' names were 1) Jack; 2) Joshua; 3) Thomas; 4) James; and 5) Daniel.

Enter the Family

One of the things that usually occurs when you have a baby is that your partner's family and your family become more involved in your lives. In some cases, 'involvement' is too mild a word. A more precise word to describe what they do might be 'interfere'. In any case, the extended family often enters the discussion about possible names.

It is not uncommon for family members to suggest a name they like. Usually (but not always) this name is a reflection of their values and past, and it is not what you had in mind for your child. One way to handle this is to be non-committal, saying that you and your partner are considering a number of names and haven't decided on anything yet. Or you may feel comfortable enough to simply say thanks, but no thanks.

You and Your Partner

Even without their direct involvement, family – hers and yours – can still participate in these naming discussions. For example, you may feel strongly that your son's name should be Joseph, a tribute to your Uncle Joe who was like a second father to you after your own father ran off to Spain with his secretary and was never heard from again. But your partner may hate that name and frankly not care all that much for Joe himself, who drinks too much and whose breath always smells of whisky.

Your partner, on the other hand, may want to choose a name that honours and reflects her parents' or grandparents' Jewish or African roots, to give just a couple of examples. Of course, she may not have said one word about her roots for all the years you two have been together. But that doesn't matter. When you have a baby, these issues suddenly come up because people identify more closely with their heritage and their past when there is a new generation on the way.

Should He Have Your Name?

One traditional male thing to do is to name your son after yourself. Some men immediately say 'no' to this concept. They have never been particularly happy with their own names, and they would not dream of weighing down their children with a similar burden.

Other men (and some women, too) want their child's name to be a reflection of their own. One byproduct of this is to feminize a first name and gave it to a daughter – Nigella, Davida, Daniella and so on.

It may be the case that your father named you after himself; the decision you and your partner must now make is whether to continue with this family tradition or break it and start a new one. You may want to talk to your own father and mother about this, if you can. Sometimes the older generation does not feel as strongly about tradition as you might think, and they want you to make your own choices.

American barbecue grill-master and former heavyweight boxing champion George Foreman solved the naming issue quite simply. He has six sons, and he named them all George – George I, II, III, IV, V and VI. It is not known what George would have done if one of his children had been a girl.

How Much Do We Tell Other People?

With just about every decision you make during pregnancy, you often have to make another decision related to it – that is, whether you should tell other people. How much do your friends and family need to know, and if you choose to tell them something, when should you do it? These are questions every couple grapples with when they have a baby.

For instance, do you tell people the due date? Letting them know the expected date of delivery helps them share the excitement of the pregnancy and plan accordingly. And yet, as the date approaches, some of these people will phone to ask whether the baby has arrived, unintentionally irritating your partner at a time when she is already feeling tense enough.

Then there is the big business of names. If you decide on your child's name, should you let others in on the secret? If you do, you possibly open yourself up to unexpected reactions from the people you are confiding in. They may not like the name you have chosen and bluntly tell you so. They may make you feel uncomfortable with a name you like, or they might put you in the middle of their naming wishes and your partner's.

Or perhaps you have not settled on a name yet and you decide to confide in your best friend with the choices you're considering. He may laugh out loud at one or two of the names you tell him – the ones you secretly like. Then what do you do? He's just doing what you asked – being honest – but you don't like his reaction.

tips

Be prepared to revisit a topic several times with your partner before making a final decision. These are big decisions, and there is no need to rush them. You both may need to talk to other people or mull things over for a while. Take as much time as you need.

Many couples reveal the due date or the name they have chosen. Others respond to questions from others with a vague answer or a more elusive one – 'The baby is due in early February' or 'We are still discussing names'. Don't let your friends or family pressure you into revealing more information than you are comfortable with. If they persist with questions you don't want to answer, simply explain that you prefer to keep that information under wraps for the time being.

Home Birth versus Hospital

Until relatively recent times, nearly all births took place at home. In many parts of the world, this is still true. In the UK, however, most couples give birth in a hospital, primarily because they feel it is safer than at home. If an emergency arises and medical intervention is required, the mother and child can receive immediate attention.

Nevertheless, some couples consider having their child at home under the guidance of a community midwife. Alternatively, you can hire an independent midwife who looks after your partner throughout pregnancy and delivers your baby at home – as long as everything goes to plan. You can expect to pay at least £2000 for this service.

The Complaints Against Hospitals

Some parents criticize hospitals for being insensitive to their needs. They feel that the hospital environment is cold and impersonal, not in tune with the 'natural' act of having a baby. They also feel that doctors and nurses sometimes follow a strict medical protocol regardless of the wishes of the parents, particularly those of the labouring mother. For these reasons and others, they choose to give birth at home.

Partly in response to such criticisms, many hospitals have made a concerted effort to be more welcoming to new parents. They have built parent-friendly labour and delivery rooms. Before they come to the hospital, each couple prepares a 'birth plan' (covered later in this chapter), which explains, in writing, how they want the birth to proceed. Midwives and doctors use this plan to guide them and – it is hoped – provide parents with a satisfying birthing experience.

Join the Discussion

The labour and delivery process for your first child will generally last longer than for your second. Some couples choose to have their first baby at a hospital. Then, after they've gone through the process once, they might choose to have their second child at home.

If you and your partner are considering having the baby at home, discuss this with your GP. You should also talk to other parents who have had home births. As your partner's birthing partner, you may feel more comfortable at a hospital with lots of medical backup close at hand. Whatever your feelings, they need to be part of the discussion.

Having the Birth You Both Want

It is important to realize that you can make choices about how you want the birth to proceed, even if you choose to give birth in a hospital. You have a voice in what goes on – assuming, that is, you use it.

Your partner may have strong opinions on certain subjects. Even though the birth is taking place in a hospital, she may want to have as natural a delivery as possible, without an epidural or pain-killing drugs. Then again, she may be afraid of the pain and want that medication as quickly as they will let her have it. It has become increasingly common for doctors to jump-start the birth by giving drugs to induce labour, rather than waiting for it to happen.

You may have strong opinions on all these subjects. You may not want to have the birth at home, if your partner is thinking along those lines. You may want her to consider pain medication and not be so dead-set against it. Or, if she's the opposite type, you may need to remind her that she will need to be in labour for a while before she receives an epidural – if it is given too early, it may stall her progress.

As your partner's birthing partner, one of your jobs is to talk to her about all these things. Think these issues through – big and small – and try to work them out together. Whatever the two of you decide, and are comfortable with, that is the way to try and do it.

Writing a Birth Plan

Despite amazing advances in technology and medical science, having a baby remains a mysterious act. So much about it is not known. No one knows, for example, what triggers the onset of labour. The full moon? The changing of the tides? Theories and superstitions abound.

Another truth about childbirth is that it is impossible to control. Things happen in the process of labour and delivery that no one can predict. Each child's birth follows a pattern similar to every other child's birth, and yet it is different too. There are lots and lots of variables.

One way that you and your partner can get a handle on these two elements – what is unknown and what cannot be controlled – is to form a birth plan. A birth plan is a one- or two-page written statement that you create with the help of your partner's midwife and give to hospital staff when you arrive to deliver the baby. Probably your partner will write the first draft of the plan. You will want to review it and discuss with her any changes you would like to suggest. Such a birth plan might include the following:

- Birth companion: who will be present besides you and your partner during labour? (Some women like to have their mother or a woman friend with them.) Does your partner want this person leave the room during specific procedures or stages in labour?
- Positions for labour and birth: what positions would your partner like to use during labour and delivery? How mobile does she want to be – up and walking for as long as she can, or staying in bed?
- Pain relief: what kinds of pain relief might she want, if any?
- Birthing pool: if the hospital has a birthing pool, or if you are hiring one for a home birth, does your partner want to use it only for pain relief or to give birth in, too?
- Foetal heart monitoring: how would you like your baby to be monitored during labour? The midwife can listen to your baby's heart intermittently using a hand-held ultrasound device, or mum can have a belt strapped round her waist, which monitors the heartbeat throughout labour.
- Delivery position: does mum wish to give birth lying on the bed, kneeling, standing up or squatting?
- Assisted delivery: if, at the end of labour, she needs some help to deliver your baby, would your partner prefer forceps or ventouse?
- Cutting the cord: do you, dad, want to cut the umbilical cord?
- First feed: does mum want to take the baby to her breast even before the cord is cut or the placenta delivered?
- Feeding baby: will baby be breastfed or bottlefed? If breastfed, state clearly whether or not baby is allowed any bottles.

A birth plan is not an absolute. As detailed and complete as your birth plan may be, you should always be prepared for the unexpected. The one thing you can count on in childbirth is that things will not proceed as planned. Be prepared, therefore, to make changes and to act on unanticipated developments.

Birth Control

Another big issue that needs to be discussed is birth control. Are you going to have another child after this one? Although it may seem extremely premature to talk about this issue, you may resume sexual relations with your partner as early as six weeks after the baby is born.

Some people believe that if a woman is breastfeeding, she cannot become pregnant. Some also believe that if a woman has not resumed menstruating after having a baby, she cannot get pregnant. Neither is true. You need to take precautions when you start having sex; otherwise, you may find yourself expecting another child sooner than planned.

Many couples decide to have more than one child. Even those who end up only having one often do not immediately know what they want to do. Having a baby can be overwhelming at first, and it takes time to work out whether you want your child to have a brother or sister.

Your partner especially will need to rest and recover after the baby comes. You will both need to make adjustments to this major new development in your lives. All of which leads back to the subject of birth control. It may be that this was an unplanned pregnancy – that your partner was on the pill or using a diaphragm when it happened. Or perhaps you happened to forget to put on a condom that night. In any case, it may be wise to review your birth control techniques and think about a different approach.

When talking with your partner about birth control or anything else, remember that not every discussion needs to lead to a plan of action or an immediate solution. Just sitting down together and airing your thoughts may be all that needs to be done at the moment.

Nappies

You have a simple decision to make here. Do you want disposable nappies, or cloth? If you and your partner choose to use cloth nappies, you may want to consider using a nappy service. The service will deliver clean nappies to you and pick up dirty ones every week. It's a good idea to start looking into what services are available in your area and what they cost now, before baby comes.

If you opt for disposable nappies, you can buy them at almost any supermarket. They are expensive, though.

There is an ongoing debate over what kind of nappy is better or worse for the environment. The cloth advocates say that disposable nappies are a menace. They are not biodegradable, and they add to the country's landfill problems. Advocates of the disposable nappy say that cloth is hardly pure, environmentally. Cleaning cloth nappies requires harsh chemicals and large amounts of water. Additionally, nappy services log plenty of miles on vehicles that use petrol and oil.

In terms of convenience and ease of use, there really is no debate. Disposables are the clear winner. You may want to give cloth nappies a try to see how you like them. You can always switch to disposables if they don't work out.

Nappies are only one of the many decisions you need to make during this time. Some decisions, such as choosing your child's name, are downright fun. Others – developing a birth plan, deciding on pain medication, the question of feeding – require thought and planning. Still other decisions, such as birth control, may need to be pondered over time. Whatever you decide on these things, the best approach is always to talk to your partner and find common ground.

Chapter 13

Preparing Your Home and Car

It makes sense to be ready for the big day. Doing a few practical things around the house or flat will help your partner relax, and it may reassure you as well. Here are some ways to prepare your home and car before the baby arrives and everything goes crazy.

The Nesting Instinct

While living with their pregnant partners, many fathers-to-be have observed what can only be described as 'the nesting instinct'. Often women focus intently on their surroundings, feeling a strong need to prepare their house or flat for the baby. Sometimes this feeling can make an expecting mother frustrated with her current abode. If she lives in a flat, she may want to try to buy a house. If she already lives in a house, she may want a bigger one.

These nesting urges on the part of your partner, while common among pregnant women, may feel like another degree of pressure squeezing in on you. If she suddenly starts talking about moving to a bigger place, this represents an obvious financial challenge. With her about to leave her job for an indefinite time due to the pregnancy and new baby, the burden of paying an increased rent or mortgage will fall largely on your shoulders, at least in the beginning. You may not be ready for a change of this magnitude, and you need to tell her that.

Your partner's nesting feelings may crop up in other ways as well. She probably does not want to go out very much at night or even at weekends. This is partly because she is tired and perhaps uncomfortable in her body, but it's also because she wants to stay at home, where she feels more comfortable. This tendency will only get stronger the closer she gets to her due date.

Men don't talk about it much, but many of them have nesting feelings too. The instinct is not nearly as strong as their partner's, perhaps, but many fathers-to-be also feel a pull towards home during the final months of pregnancy. To some degree, this is due to the needs of the mother, who wants the father-to-be close by and able to respond if something happens. This is a time when many men cancel or postpone work-related trips that may take them far from home.

These nesting feelings serve a valuable purpose. They motivate both you and your partner to get your home in order. You do not have to move into a mansion or build a new wing on the house because you are having a baby. But a few simple things need to be taken care of. Once they have been, you and your partner will feel more at ease.

Preparing the Nursery

From the man's point of view, one nice thing about getting the nursery ready is that you actually get to do something. For the father-to-be, so much of the pregnancy consists of waiting... and waiting... and waiting. Not much happens directly to you, and there is not much to do. Preparing the nursery gives you a chance to open a tin of paint and get your hands dirty.

What if my partner wants to do something I don't like?
Let her know, but give her an alternative. If you know you're having a boy, and she wants to paint the nursery lilac, suggest that a more gender-neutral colour, such as yellow or green, may be more appropriate. She will be more open to you if she doesn't feel criticized.

Many parents-to-be, of course, do not have a separate room for a nursery. They make do by using a portion of their own bedroom or another room. This may not be ideal, but it works just fine, and the baby doesn't care at all. He and all the gear related to him are basically going to take over your whole place anyway.

Reporting for Duty

It may be that you are an interior decorator at heart and have elaborate ideas on the colours and look of your baby's nursery. It is more likely, however, that you have not given this subject one thought in your entire life. Almost certainly, your partner will take the lead in this area, and you will follow. She will be the head designer and make the big decisions. You will be the labourer. So it goes.

Expect there to be several changes to her design scheme before she settles on a final look. She may want to sample different paint colours to see which ones she likes. She may want to call in outside consultants – her mother and friends – to help her with her decision-making process. She will probably ask you what you think.

For many women, putting together their child's nursery is a little like planning a wedding. They have certain ideas and expectations on how they want things to be. And they feel these things quite strongly and occasionally show their emotions.

Safety First

While you may be willing to go along with your partner's design scheme for the nursery, the one area that you cannot be silent about is safety. The safety of your child's surroundings is your number-one consideration. It takes precedence over everything else.

Painting and preparing the nursery is a good middle-trimester project, say around the sixth or seventh month. Paint the nursery well in advance of the baby's arrival – you want the room to be aired completely before she has to sleep in it. You do not want her breathing harmful fumes.

Safety Checklist

Most nursery injuries occur when the child is older and can move around. Your child will not be able to jump or bounce or move around for some months. You will put her down on her back, and that is how she will be when you return to pick her up after her nap. Even so, the nursery needs to be safe from day one.

To begin with, your baby will probably sleep in a Moses basket, carry cot or newborn crib – full-size cots seem far too vast for that tiny scrap of baby. But just you wait. In three or for months he'll be outgrowing that cute first bed and you'll need to move him. It's vital that you check any cot that you borrow or buy for safety. Look for the following features:

· The cot feels sturdy and stable and if it has castors, these lock securely.
· Its surfaces are smooth with no sharp protrusions; the slats are no more than 7.5cm (3in) apart; and there are no decorative cutouts that could trap the baby's head.

- If it has corner posts, these are 0.15cm (1/16 in) or less (any higher and a jumping baby catching clothing on the post risks strangulation).
- The mattress is firm and fits snugly (less than two fingers' width between mattress and side).
- There is no soft, fluffy bedding, such as pillows, duvets or sheepskins, as these pose a risk of suffocation.
- The cot is nowhere near a window, heater, lamp, wall decoration, cord (curtain or light) or climbable furniture.

Many parents simply pop a plastic changing mat on their bed for nappy changing. Others buy a changing table. Whichever way you go, you want to keep the baby from falling off. Custom-made changing tables often come with an integral safety strap. Baby wipes, cotton wool and creams need to be in easy reach – you don't want to leave the baby unattended on the bed or table while you walk across the room for supplies.

The Family Bed

An increasing number of couples do not use a Moses basket or crib. They let their newborn sleep in bed with them. This is called 'the family bed' – Mum, Dad and baby, all sleeping together.

How does this work out? Well, it depends on the family. Some fathers love sleeping with their infant children. They may be away at work and not see their family all day long. Being able to share a bed with them at night makes them feel connected to them.

Family bed advocates believe that it promotes family togetherness as well as a greater sense of well-being for the child. The child is not alone in a crib or Moses basket; she is cuddled up with her mother and father, sharing their bodily warmth. This, say the family bed people, comforts her and makes her feel more secure. Some parents like sleeping with their child because it is truly something you can only do when she is little. When she grows older and bigger, she will have to move into a crib.

Many men, however, are not too keen on the family bed concept. They are often the ones who have to get up early in the morning to go to work.

They need a good night's sleep – as good as they can get, anyway – and they do not want to hear every peep and cry and gurgle their newborn makes. Family beds frequently turn into fatherless beds because the man leaves to sleep on the sofa or in the spare room.

Men worry about possibly rolling over on top of their child. Even if it doesn't happen, the thought of it causes them to lose sleep. Some men also see their time in bed with their partners as precious. Even if they do not make love, they can talk and be intimate with her. The baby's presence in bed can interfere with this.

Never let your newborn sleep on a waterbed. The mattress should be firm, with no folds or spaces in the bedding that might affect her breathing. Remember that alcohol can deaden your senses when you are asleep. **NEVER** sleep in the same bed with an infant after you've been drinking. And you should never share a bed with your baby if either of you smokes, as this increases the risk of cot death.

If either you or your partner cares to sleep with the baby, you may want to give it a try to see how it works. One advantage is that when the baby cries in the middle of the night and needs to be fed, neither of you has to stand up to get him. Your partner slips him her breast, and he quiets down. A bedside bed could be a good compromise. This is a cot that can be adapted to fit next to your partner's side of the bed with one side removed. When the baby has finished nursing, Mum slides her onto her own bed, allowing her to be close to the two of you but in a separate space.

Babyproofing Your Home

Fortunately, this is one thing you do not need to worry about during pregnancy. Your baby is tucked safely inside his mother's body and cannot yet crawl around and pull books out of the bookshelf or fiddle with the knobs on your CD player. This is something you have to look forward to.

You can easily wait until your baby is two to four months old before childproofing your home. Basically, you want to make sure that where you live is a safe environment for your child to move around in and explore. Here are a few childproofing basics:

- Move objects on shelves out of child's reach.
- Attach childproof latches to drawers you do not want your child to get into.
- Install safety gates at top and bottom of stairs.
- Attach corner pads to sharp-edged tables and furniture.
- Put on cooker knob covers and other oven safety devices. Use the back burners when cooking on the stove.
- Install a toilet guard so the child cannot lift the lid.
- Insert socket covers in all electrical outlets.
- Put breakable dishes out of reach or lock them up.
- Make sure all medicine, cleaning products, garden fertilizer and pesticides are locked up and out of reach.
- Install large, childproof fireguards around open or other fires.

Childproof products are available at hardware stores, supermarkets, specialist children's shops and many other places. Once your child begins to move around, you will be amazed at how creative he will be at getting into potentially hazardous situations. Take your eyes off him for one second, and suddenly he's into something he shouldn't be. That is why childproofing is necessary.

In the Event of an Emergency

Accidents are the leading cause of injury and death among children, far exceeding disease and illness. The causes include electric shock, drowning, swallowing foreign objects or poisonous substances, fire, burns and car crashes. Close calls and accidents of any kind will require fast thinking and action on your part.

Infant Resuscitation

Most parents will never have to use resuscitation techniques on their children. But babies are putting things in their mouth all the time –

things they find on the carpet, things they find in the garden – and they can easily choke. Babies can accidentally fall into a pool or shallow water and be unable to get out. Babies can also experience breathing difficulties at times.

Pregnancy is a good time to take an infant resuscitation class because you're motivated to learn as much as you can. You may even be a little scared. This fear is a good thing if it inspires you to learn the ABCs – airway, breathing, circulation – of emergency life-resuscitation techniques.

Certainly your childminder, if you use one, needs to know how to perform resuscitation on an infant. It should be one of the questions you ask before you leave your child with her. She should take a refresher course every year to keep up to date.

Infant resuscitation classes are widely available through local branches of the British Red Cross Society (BRCS) at www.redcross.org.uk; tel 020 7235 5454 and St John Ambulance at www.sja.org.uk; tel: 08700 104950. Classes are frequently held in the evenings and on Saturdays in order to make it easier for working parents to attend.

Preventing Burns

One safety measure you can take now (or soon after the baby comes) is to turn down the thermostat on your water heater. Most water heaters are normally set at around 60°C (155°F). By turning yours down to about 49°C (125°F), you can help prevent scalding your baby in bath water that's too hot – a common form of injury to babies.

Many burns to young children are caused not by fire but by scalding. Be careful about where you set your morning cup of coffee – a baby could knock it over and burn herself. In addition to the bath, the kitchen is a place where burn accidents frequently occur. Hot water can boil over and spill, and grease can splatter. Always be aware of where your child is.

Be wary of microwave ovens. Heating baby formula or baby food in a microwave is a bad idea. The outside of the jar can feel cool to the touch while the contents inside are boiling.

Fire Prevention

Fire prevention is another precaution you can take right now. Firefighters recommend that you test your smoke alarms every month and that you change the batteries once a year. You and your partner may have already discussed an escape route in the event of a fire in your home. If not, take a minute and talk it over.

Simple carelessness can cause a fire. Be sure you don't put a space heater too close to the curtains or wall. The kitchen is where many fires start. When you cook, turn the pot handles to the side or towards the back of the stove so a small child's hands cannot reach them. A fire extinguisher in the kitchen is recommended, as well as one kept perhaps in an upstairs bedroom.

Another thing worth checking up on is your household insurance cover. Are you adequately covered if you suffered a major loss? Now may be the time to upgrade your policy.

Staying in Touch: Mobile Phones

Mobile phones were invented for pregnant couples to stay in touch with each other. Well, OK, that may be stretching it a little, but they are useful during this time. If you do not yet have mobile phones, you may want to look into getting them.

Not long ago, birthing partners were advised to bring lots of coins with them when they came to the hospital for labour and delivery. After the birth, they made their calls from the pay phone in the hallway to let people know that the baby had arrived. In most hospitals they still do, as you are not allowed to switch mobiles on in hospital buildings. But you can always go out to the car park and call from there – or use the old-fashioned call box!

Another advantage to mobile phones is that they let you keep in touch with your partner as you get closer and closer to the big day. She may want to check in with you frequently, and vice versa. If you work in a place where you're not always close to a land line, mobile phones can be real gems.

Mobile phones are obviously useful in emergencies as well. If you've had a panicky call from your partner telling you that she has gone into labour and needs you to come home right away, you can respond instantaneously. Then, when your car breaks down on the way home, you can call her and tell her you're going to be a few minutes late.

Car Seats

Car seats are not just options; they are a true necessity. You need a car seat to take your child home from the hospital. The hospital staff is required to check for one or at least ask you about it before releasing the baby into your care.

It is wise to install your car seat a few days or a week before the due date. You never know what can happen, and if your partner goes into labour and you need to go to the hospital unexpectedly, the car seat is one less thing you have to think about.

Child safety seats are credited with saving thousands of lives over the years. Safety experts believe that even more lives could be saved if more parents learned to install these seats correctly. Studies have shown that nine out of ten car seats are improperly installed, exposing babies and infants to unnecessary risk.

Car Seat Basics

Your baby's weight determines the type of safety seat to use. For an infant of up to 13kg (29lb), use a rear-facing infant seat. At about the age of one, your child may go over this weight, at which point you can switch to a car seat that faces forwards. The car seat should be placed in the back seat, and the baby gets buckled into that.

Some vehicles have passenger-side air bags. These can be extremely dangerous if a child is placed in a rear-facing car seat in the front seat. When the bag inflates, it can hit the back of the car seat, push it forward, and injure the child. Always buckle your child in his car seat in the back seat – the safest spot is behind the driver.

Sometimes the car seat does not work with the existing seat belt. You may need to buy a supplemental belt or a locking clip. Never improvise with a car seat. If it doesn't work properly, get one that does.

Find Out How to Install

Child safety seats would seem to be easy to install, but often they are not. Sometimes it is difficult to work out how to work the car seat's straps and buckles. The child must be strapped into the car seat, and that must be held in place by the seat belt. It can be confusing. For more information, go to www.childcarseats.org.uk.

Your local police and fire stations may be able to help you install your car seat. Or, if you've got it in, they can check to see that you've done it correctly. Childbirth preparation classes sometimes offer this service. If yours doesn't, the teachers can still tell you where to get help.

Sometimes hospitals hold seminars for pregnant couples and invite police officers to check over the installation of car seats. This is usually a popular attraction for fathers-to-be. It is frequently their job to put in the car seat, and they want to make sure they do it properly.

Chapter 14

Birthing Partner

A father has many important jobs in a family. He is a provider, guardian, teacher, advisor, role model, disciplinarian and nurturer. These days, fathers-to-be have an added responsibility: birthing partner. This chapter explains what you need to know to help your partner bring your child into the world.

What a Birthing Partner Does

Millions of fathers have served as birthing partners. These men would testify that it is one of the greatest experiences they have ever had. To see your child draw her first breath of air and to assist in her delivery – there is nothing quite like it in the world. It is demanding, nerve-wracking, exhausting, frustrating, emotionally draining – and one of the greatest natural highs a man can have. If you miss your child's birth, these men will tell you, you are truly missing out on one of life's most rewarding and enriching experiences.

Many fathers have qualms before the birth. Having only heard about it and never done it before, they may have privately wondered if they were up to the task. Once they went through it, though, they realized that they had basically been worried about nothing. They handled it perfectly well.

Be Her Supporters' Club and Representative

The title of birthing partner is actually a misnomer. You're more of a cheerleader than a partner. While the midwife gets on with ensuring a safe delivery, you cheer your partner on by offering encouragement in her ear and telling her you love her.

Being a cheerleader is not your only job, however. Far from it. You have other, equally important jobs. One of them is serving as your partner's chief advocate, her voice amidst all the activity that is going on around her.

'What's that?' you may say. 'My partner has never had any trouble speaking up for herself in the past. Why does she need me to speak for her in the most important moments of her life?'

The simple answer is that she may not be able to. She may be in so much pain she cannot think straight. She may be angry or in tears or feel as if things are out of control. The nurses may have given her drugs to combat the pain, and those drugs may have made her light-headed. Various scenarios can arise in which the medical team needs to consult with you.

You and your partner have talked about how you want the delivery to proceed. You know what her wishes are. You have prepared a birth plan together. You may have her sister or a private midwife in the room with you. All this will help guide you as you deal with the hospital staff.

You can disagree with the medical staff if you do not like what is going on. The labour may have stalled, and the staff may suggest giving your partner a drug you've never heard of. They may warn that if things don't pick up, she is destined for a caesarean section. But you may decide to stick to your guns, telling them that you are going to keep working with your partner and doing the activities that you learned in childbirth classes to stimulate the labour and get it moving again.

You must strike a balance when dealing with the medical staff. You are not a trained midwife or doctor. You have never been through this before; they have. But you do have a voice and some power in this situation. Ultimately, though, the attending medics will make the final decisions.

Your Baby's Chief Advocate

You also have an important role on behalf of your unborn child. Sometimes you are her chief advocate, too.

Your partner may have requested an epidural in her birth plan. But epidurals are only given at a certain stage in the labour. They should not be administered too early, nor can they be administered beyond a certain point. In your partner's case, her labour may have moved so fast that an epidural is no longer called for. But she can still be in extreme pain and yelling for one.

The nurses may advise you, however, that providing pain relief drugs for your partner at this point may slow the labour down and affect the baby's progress down the birth canal. You must do the right thing for your child, even if it contradicts the wishes of your partner. Tell her what is going on and why. Be sure she knows that the pain she is feeling is productive pain and that she is getting results. Then work with her and support her and help her to get that baby out.

You will probably be called upon to make decisions in the labour and delivery room. That is the nature of your job as birthing partner. It is not a passive role. You may be exhausted and a little light-headed and not exactly sure what the right thing to do is. Still, with the assistance of the medical team, you make a judgment and go with it.

Antenatal Classes

As the name implies, antenatal classes are designed to get you and your partner ready for labour and delivery. These classes may help reduce the fear and worry and give you a sense of what you can expect.

Your hospital or local National Childbirth Trust (NCT) will probably offer these classes. You'll usually attend these classes in the seventh or eighth month of the pregnancy. Classes are held once a week for six to ten weeks. Note that if you want to attend NCT classes you should book as soon as your partner gets pregnant, as classes are in great demand.

One purpose of these classes is to provide information and teach you about the process of childbirth. Some men may assume that their partners know everything there is to know about their bodies and what happens when they have a baby. This is rarely the case. Your partner may be as clueless about all of this as you are, giving you both the chance to learn together.

Indeed, this is another purpose of these classes: to foster a connection between you and your partner. You are going to have to learn how to work as a team. Another way to put it is that the two of you got into this together. Now you are going to have to get through it together, too.

Supporting Mum Physically

Another major reason for attending childbirth preparation classes is the specific techniques you learn to help your partner endure the pain of labour and delivery as well as she possibly can. If you want an inkling of what it is like to have a baby, go out into the garage and stick your thumb in a vice. Then tighten the vice, loosen it, and then tighten it again and then loosen it, each time tightening it harder than the last. Keep doing this for, oh, the next 24 to 36 hours straight, and you will still not be close to feeling the pain of a woman in labour – because it is not just her thumb that is absorbing this ever-tightening, vice-like pain, it's her whole body.

To help her get through this ordeal, your partner is going to learn some breathing and other techniques to relax and endure the pain. Your job will be to assist her. You can help her in a variety of ways, including these:

· Walking with her, keeping her moving.
· Encouraging her to sit up, not labour lying down.
· Letting her lean on you while standing, her arms around your neck to take some of the pressure off her legs.
· Applying counter-pressure, with your hand against her lower back during a contraction.
· Helping her in and out of the water if she wants to take a bath.
· Letting her lean on you in the shower as the hot water hits her lower back.
· Getting her glasses of water, because she will be expending a lot of energy and needs to keep her fluids up.
· Applying a cold flannel to her forehead.

These techniques probably work best during early labour. Later, when labour progresses and the pain becomes more intense, it is going to be more difficult to find ways to assist her. Her focus is intensely inward, and there are many new sensations occurring inside her body. You may find that many of the techniques you learned in childbirth preparation class are useless and that they provide no comfort to her. But you won't know that until you're in the middle of things.

Listen to your partner. She will tell you what she needs. Light massage may help her initially, or it may not. Or it may help in the beginning, but as the labour goes on, she may tell you that your touch irritates and distracts her. Don't take anything personally, just try to respond in the moment and do the best you can.

Providing Emotional Support

As the labour goes on (and on and on) and the pain keeps riding the up escalator, the emotional support you give your partner may be the most important thing you can do for her. First labours are almost never as quick as second labours: they can last for 12 to 16 to 24 to 36 hours. Obviously, the longer it drags on, the more exhausted and discouraged your partner will be.

In the face of all this, your job is to tell her what a great job she is doing, how much you love her, how hard she is working, how proud you are of her and how much progress she is making. Your goal is to buck up her spirits and keep her going. Make sure she knows she is not alone and that you are with her all the way.

The Hospital Visit

A standard part of antenatal classes is the hospital tour. Led by a midwife, you and your partner and the rest of your class get a tour of the maternity wing. Although it may feel a little like being shepherded around by your teacher on a primary school outing, it's worth going. The tour will give you a feel for the place where your child will be born.

As the instructor leads you around, she will fill you in on hospital dos and don'ts. One issue you need to be aware of is where to park the car while you're checking your partner into her room. If it's a small hospital, you may be able to simply park in the car park and walk her in. But in larger hospitals, the only parking available is sometimes in a giant multi-storey car park some distance away from the maternity wing. In this case, you may have to park temporarily near the maternity unit, then check in your partner and get her settled before going back out to park your car.

Wheelchair for Pregnant Mums

Every hospital has its own way of doing things, but it is generally recommended that the labouring mother ride in a wheelchair once she arrives. Some women in labour resist. They say they do not need it, and they can walk quite happily. And many do indeed walk all the way to the labour wards, steadying themselves on a railing along the wall.

Sometimes you may need to insist that your partner do something that you feel she should. Other times you will need to back off and help her do it the way she wants to. You will both be stressed in these moments. Becoming defensive or sulking because you did not get your way will not help the situation.

Depending on the stage of her labour, your partner may be struggling as she walks, stopping whenever the pain of a contraction comes on. You might suggest to her that she is going to be working awfully hard over the next hours, and there is no reason why she cannot take it easy and accept a ride in a wheelchair. If she still says no, just help her as best as you can.

The Admitting Room

After parking your car and winding your way through to the hospital, at some point you will reach the admitting room. You have already phoned ahead to the hospital to let them know you're coming, so they have already got out your partner's medical chart. You are carrying copies of your birth plan, so you give one to the nurse to attach to the chart. The admitting room is where the hospital will decide whether to book you a room for the night.

Don't be surprised if the nurse tells you, 'Sorry, your partner's cervix is not dilated enough. Go back home, keep waiting, and call us in a few hours.' As frustrating as that may be, it happens quite frequently, particularly for first-time mothers. More about this is discussed in Chapters 15 and 16.

The Labour and Delivery Room

Once you've been admitted, you and your partner will be assigned a labour and delivery room. One or more of the nurses will take your case and work with you and your partner.

First labours can last a long time. One nurse may be on duty when you arrive. But sooner or later, she will go off duty and another nurse will take her place. Your partner could still be in labour, 18 to 24 hours later, when your original nurse comes back on duty the next day. It is not uncommon to work with several different nurses over the course of a single labour and delivery.

More Stops on the Tour

Another stop on the hospital tour is the lunch or beverage room. Your partner may never see this room while she is in labour, but you will probably visit it several times. You can use this room to get ice cubes for your partner (some women like to suck them to quench their thirst) and ice-cold water from a refrigerated dispenser. There is likely to be a hot-water pot for coffee or tea, and a refrigerator where birthing partners can store their food.

Sometimes on the tour they take you past the door of the neonatal intensive care unit. Premature babies and babies who have problems at birth are brought to this room, where they are cared for by highly trained, dedicated and motivated specialist physicians and nurses. You will not be allowed to go into this room, and you may not even want to think about any circumstances in which your child would have to go there. But it is comforting to know that if anything does happen, the neonatal ICU is close to hand.

The Nursery

The nursery is the show-stopping highlight of most hospital tours. It is where the newborns are kept if they are not in the room with Mum. Everybody on the tour stands outside the window, grinning like idiots. Even at this late date in the pregnancy, it is still hard to fathom that you and your partner are soon going to have one of those babies soon.

What to Bring to the Hospital

Television sitcoms and films often rely on standard jokes when they tell stories involving women in labour and the well-meaning but bumbling men in their life. One of these jokes has to do with a woman who is having big contractions and needs to go to the hospital – pronto! In his haste and confusion, the father jumps into the car and drives off without her. Only after he is on the road does he realize his mistake.

One reason why this scenario never occurs in real life is that it is impossible to forget about your labouring partner. She will not let you drive off without her. Here are some other items that you dare not forget when you take your partner to the hospital to have a baby:

- A bag of essentials, including your birth plan, your partner's dressing gown and slippers and a pair of warm bed socks (her feet can get very cold in labour), an old comfy nightdress to wear in labour, toiletries.
- A bag of extras that you and she have decided to bring, such as massage oils or lotions, lip moisturizer, snacks and drinks for both of you, a camera and film/tape, books, magazines, games and music.
- A change of clothes for you.
- Items for your partner after the birth: breastfeeding bras, breast pads, sanitary towels, clean nightie.
- Address book, plus lots of change or a prepaid phone card for all the calls you may want to make. You are unlikely to be allowed to use your mobile phone in the hospital building.
- You will need to bring in some things for the new baby, too. Few hospitals provide baby clothes, nighties or nappies these days. So bring several little bodysuit vests and a couple of stretchy babygros, and a bag of newborn disposable nappies. For the trip home baby will need a hat, a warm outdoor suit if it's winter or a cardigan in summer, a shawl or baby blanket.
- Last but not least, pack a set of going-home clothes for your partner; and most importantly, an infant car seat.

You need to dress comfortably – you may be in those clothes for a long time. Wear good trainers or shoes that give you plenty of support because you will be on your feet a lot. Giving birth is a kind of marathon. You need to prepare yourself for the long haul, and bring whatever you need to help you and your partner make it to the finish line.

Asking a Family Member to Assist You

Many fathers who have served as birthing partners heartily recommend bringing in another person to assist during labour and delivery. It is another pair of hands that can help out during this turbulent time. If the labour goes on for many hours, you can cover for each other when one of you needs a break. This person can also provide valuable counsel. If a decision needs to be made, it is often useful to hear the opinion of someone you know and who knows you well, too.

Make sure your co-partner is a team player who will work together with you. Avoid high-maintenance personalities who may agitate or upset you or your partner.

Some fathers who served as their partner's only labour companion for their first child choose to bring in another person for the birth of their second child. They know from experience that labour can be an overwhelming experience and that another person in the room can be extremely useful. In a sentence, it makes their job easier.

An obvious candidate for your birth team is someone from your partner's family – her sister or perhaps her mother. Or your partner may have a friend whom she feels close to. First talk to this person to see if she is interested. While she probably does not need to attend classes, if she has never participated in childbirth before, she may need to do some homework on the subject. The three of you will need to get together at least once before the birth to plot strategy and be clear about your roles.

Hiring a Birth Attendant

Another option worth considering is hiring a doula, or professional labour assistant. The word 'doula' derives from the Greek, meaning 'in service'. This is a good explanation of what a doula does. She is employed to be in service to your partner and you, helping you in a variety of non-medical ways.

A doula is not a medical person – she attends along with the midwife, not instead of the midwife. She is not trained in medicine, nor can she advise you on medical matters. She is not a hospital employee. She is hired by you to provide physical and emotional support during the birthing experience. The cost of this service usually ranges from £250 to £500.

Doulas are relatively new in the UK. Your partner's midwife or antenatal teacher may be able to put you in touch with one in your area, or contact the UK Doula Association (www.doula.org.uk) to see if there is one who works in your area.

What a Doula Does

Doulas cite evidence that when they are present at births, labour tends to be shorter, there are far fewer drugs used, forceps delivery occurs much less, and the caesarean rate is cut virtually in half. They say that their presence can make the labour less arduous and provide a better birthing experience for women. Doulas are almost all women, and they are frequently mothers who decided to become birth assistants after going through childbirth themselves. Most have assisted at dozens of births.

What does a doula do? She helps the mother focus on her breathing and concentration. She gets her to sit up in bed and change positions in order to keep labour progressing. She will bring a bag of birthing aids to assist the mother. One of these may be a birthing ball, which the mother can use in numerous ways, including supporting her body during a contraction. A doula may also bring hot and cold packs with her and know massage techniques, knowing where to apply counter-pressure during contractions.

How the Doula Supports You

You may be thinking, 'Why do I need to pay someone to do stuff I can do myself?' Many men also worry that a doula will take over their job.

The truth is, you are going to get tired and possibly frustrated, and a doula may be able to employ methods and techniques of moving the labour along that you are not aware of. She is a woman, probably a mother, and she knows what your partner is going through. She is also a non-medical person with experience, and you can confide in her. The doula will be an assistant to your partner and you, not someone who is there to run the show.

You may need to take a break from time to time but not want to leave your partner alone. You may have had to leave your car illegally parked and, after checking your partner into the hospital, you may not have even had five minutes to go back downstairs and move your car to the hospital car park where it should be. Having a doula (or family member) assisting in the birth gives you more freedom and flexibility and takes some of the weight off your shoulders.

A birth partner has a lot of responsibility. He is his partner's main supporter and her chief advocate at the hospital. He must support her physically and emotionally. He must sometimes make decisions on her behalf as well as his unborn child's. With everything that is going on, you may want to enlist a family member or hire a trained birth attendant to help make the birth experience as smooth as possible.

Chapter 15

The Big Day Arrives

It is here! The big day has finally arrived, the day that you have been planning for and thinking about for months. In these pages you find out what to do when your partner goes into labour, and the countdown to your baby begins.

Getting Labour Started

In many pregnancies, especially first ones, there comes a time when you think the baby is never going to arrive. In the heady early days, perhaps, the pregnancy sped along quickly. But at the ninth month, the wait for baby seems to slow down. It's like watching grass grow.

The due date comes and goes, and still there is no baby. The anticipation is hard on you, but it is much harder on your partner. They gave her a going-away party at work, but that was weeks ago. Since then she has been knocking around the house, trying to think about something other than the baby. It's been impossible.

She's been tired, more tired than ever. She doesn't even want to go outside any more, what with total strangers coming up to her at the market and feeling her belly. 'When is the bun coming out of the oven?' they ask her, thinking they're making a joke. Meanwhile, her family has cranked up the pressure by phoning the house and asking if anything has happened yet.

The number of induced births in the UK – in which women are given drugs to bring on labour – is about 20 per cent, or one in five. Interestingly, this is a similar figure to the number of women having caesarean deliveries (22 per cent).

People do a variety of things to try to jump-start those contractions on their own. Sexual intercourse might help. It is thought to work in two ways, first by triggering the release of a contraction hormone called oxytocin, and second, because semen contains prostaglandins, substances that help to soften the neck of the womb ready for it to dilate when contractions start. Stimulating your partner's nipples also seems to help with this softening process.

Simply encouraging her to walk may help your partner's labour to begin. When she walks, the baby's head presses down on the cervix from inside, stimulating the release of oxytocin. Do not let her be tempted to take laxatives. She could end up in pain and suffering from dehydration.

The Stages of Labour

If you go by what you see on television or in films, labour takes about five minutes. First the woman feels something, and then the couple is madly racing to the hospital. Then you see the woman grunting and pushing, and the baby pops out. Just like that.

For normal first-time pregnancies, it almost never goes so quickly or smoothly. Second pregnancies are different; those labours can go relatively quickly. But if this is your partner's first, count on it taking a long time – 8, to 12, to 18, to 24 hours or more.

Early Labour

Many people liken labour and delivery to a marathon race. This is an apt comparison because both go on for a long time, and all of the participants need to be prepared to go the distance. Mum needs to keep her fluid levels up just like a marathon runner, and she and her 'coach' (that's you) both need to preserve their strength so they can make it all the way.

Early labour is the beginning stage of the marathon. It can last for many hours. It can begin early in the afternoon and continue through the night. Much, if not all, of early labour will likely occur while you are still at home. It is also unlikely to be especially uncomfortable.

How do we know when early labour begins? The surest sign is that your partner's contractions begin to occur at regular intervals, less than ten minutes apart. She will probably notice this over a period of time and mention it to you. Her contractions will gradually become stronger, longer, and occur more frequently. This is a really exciting time for you both – it's really happening!

Active Labour

Active labour is the second major phase in the process. It usually occurs over a shorter time span than early labour. It may last only a couple of hours, although it may seem like an eternity to your partner, because this is when it starts to hurt. Usually you head to the hospital early in the active labour stage.

During labour, the woman's cervix gradually opens, or 'dilates', and thins out, or 'effaces'. Her cervix must be completely effaced and dilated to 10cm (4in) before she can begin to push the baby out – and, ultimately, give birth. Her contractions are the means her body uses to dilate and efface her cervix and move the baby towards birth.

In early labour, contractions can last 30 to 45 seconds or sometimes less. They are relatively mild – nothing like as strong as what will come later, and some women may not even notice them for a while. Active labour is when the contractions get kicked up a notch. They last up to a minute or so, and your partner will definitely feel them, big-time.

Early labour may dilate your partner's cervix up to 3 (1⅛in), and active labour will bring it to around 6 to 7cm (2⅜ to 2¾in). Such considerations – how far your partner is effaced and how many centimetres she is dilated – will seem like abstractions to you until you get involved in the labour. But you will quickly realize their importance. The two of you are trying to reach a goal, and those numbers will tell you how close you are to getting there.

Transition

Transition is the next big phase of labour, and it is the wildest and most intense by far. Everything kicks into hyper-drive. The contractions last 60 to 90 seconds and are very intense, with the woman climbing Himalayan peaks of pain. Contractions take place every two to three minutes. Your partner will barely get a chance to recover from the last wave before another one, perhaps of greater intensity, washes over her.

If a mother in labour pushes too soon, it can slow down delivery. One of your jobs is to help her fight the urge to push. Tell her to blow or pant with her breath. Help her with any breathing techniques she may have learned. Slow, even breaths between contractions may relax her.

Transition can last anywhere from 15 minutes to an hour. It is like the sprint to the finish line. It is during transition that the cervix reaches the promised land of 10cm (4in), allowing the woman to push. This is when she may swear at you for getting her in this state in the first place.

Pushing

Next comes pushing, which will be discussed in greater detail in Chapter 16. Unlike what you see in films or on television, pushing is not a matter of a few quick grunts and you're done. It can last an hour and a half or more. When it's time to push, you – and especially your partner – still have a lot of work left to do.

Even so, most mothers in labour welcome the chance to push. Although it is still painful and they are utterly exhausted by this time, being able to push gives them a sense of control that they lacked during transition and earlier in the labour. At long last, they get to assert themselves and do something to birth their baby.

Early Signs of Progress

Early in the pregnancy, your partner experienced what are called Braxton Hicks contractions. These are sort of practice contractions that slowly get her body ready to deliver the baby. As the due date nears, these contractions can become stronger and more frequent though not painful, but they are usually only a warm-up act for the real thing. One of the surest signs of real labour – as opposed to 'false labour' or, more accurately, prelabour – is that your partner's contractions become regular.

There are other signs that labour may be beginning. One is called 'the show'. This is when the mucus plug, which acts like a cork in the cervix, gets discharged, accompanied by a little blood. Your partner will almost certainly tell you when this occurs. If you are at work, you may receive a phone call telling you to come home or at least be prepared for action.

The show, however, does not necessarily mean that labour is imminent. It could be, of course, but it is impossible to say for sure. After the mucus plug comes unglued, a day or two will sometimes pass before the woman starts her labour.

For some women, the first sign that labour is on the way is when their 'waters' break. The amniotic sac that protects the foetus has broken, and labour (if it hasn't started already) will probably occur within 12 to 24 hours, possibly sooner. Sometimes the waters can break while she is asleep in the middle of the night, and this can be quite shocking. Some may experience it as a slight trickle of fluids that they need to investigate.

But again, there are many variations. Some women experience labour contractions for hours and hours before their waters break. With others, their waters break but they do not begin contractions for a day or more. When a midwife or doctor induces labour, one of the steps she may take is to artificially rupture the membranes.

Once the waters break, most obstetricians want labour to begin within 24 hours. If it has not, they will use prostaglandin gel on the cervix or other means to stimulate the start of labour. The waters have served as a barrier to possible infection, and the baby cannot safely stay in the womb for too long without that protection. When the waters do break, contact the maternity ward for advice on whether to come in at once or to wait a while.

Keeping Early Labour Moving Along

Once labour begins for real, you want to make steady progress towards your goal. While the pain will never be easy for your partner to endure, she will feel better if she sees that her contractions are producing results – that is, if her cervix is continuing to dilate and efface. It is frustrating for you both when labour stalls, and all the hard work she is doing appears to be achieving nothing.

This is where you, as birthing partner, can play a valuable role. During early labour, when the two of you are at home, there are some things you can do to help keep things moving along, such as these:

· Take a gentle walk with her.
· Encourage her to sit up. (Lying down will slow labour.)

- Prepare a bath for her (if her waters haven't broken yet) or a shower.
- Massage her shoulders or back.
- Bring out the birthing ball and let her lean her body over it while she is having a contraction.
- Find ways to help her relax and distract her mind by playing cards or a board game or watching television.

Rest and relaxation are essential for both of you. You probably have a long way to go before the baby is born, so pace yourselves. Although you both want to make progress, be a calming influence on your partner. Encourage her. Tell her what a great job she is doing. Putting pressure on her will only cause her to tense up, and this will delay progress.

tips

One of your jobs will be to time your partner's contractions. Use a wristwatch with a second hand. The timing starts from the beginning of one contraction and extends to the beginning of the next, including the rest period in between. You should probably go to the hospital when you see that her contractions are occurring about five minutes apart or less.

Things You Need to Do

It is likely that at some point during the pregnancy you have felt useless and basically irrelevant to the whole process. You're not alone if you've felt like this. But almost certainly, at that moment when your partner goes into labour – the real thing – all your feelings of being unneeded or unwanted disappear in a heartbeat. There are suddenly lots of things to do, and you are just the person to do them.

Stay Calm

Your partner is going through something she has never gone through before. She has no idea what she is about to experience. It's natural that she may feel a rush of emotions – happiness, relief, fear, anxiety – when labour finally kicks in. Adding to these feelings will be the pain that wracks her body every time a contraction comes on.

You will also feel a variety of emotions. You are going to be excited and happy and relieved as well. At long last, things are finally happening. You may have had a call from your partner to come home from work. You may have already been at home when the contractions started. Her labour may have started in the middle of the night, waking you from a sound sleep.

Whatever your specific situation, the rule at this point is simple. Be cool and calm. Depending on who she is and how she responds to the pain she is feeling, your partner may be having a rough time. You can best serve her by being someone she can lean on, physically and emotionally.

The Importance of Rest

Whatever time of day your partner's contractions started, you can almost count on her to be in labour well into the night. There is a theory that the reason so many women labour at night dates back to prehistoric times. When they gave birth, cave women needed a safe, secure place in which they could feel protected. At night, under cover of darkness, they were less exposed to potential danger. You may laugh at this theory, but it is pretty certain that you will lose at least one night of sleep during labour.

Because labour can last so long, and because it often extends overnight, it is important to rest. Your partner needs to rest and relax as much as possible between contractions. As crazy as it may sound, she may need to go back to bed to see if she can sleep. She will soon need all the strength and energy she can muster.

This is true for you, too. You need to pace yourself and try to rest, even if the contractions are occurring during the day. Remember that labour is like running a marathon. It's a long, gruelling ordeal, and you want to be as alert as possible all the way to the end.

Use Your Nervous Energy

Realistically, however, when your partner goes into contractions, you are not going to excuse yourself to go and have a nap. You will have lots of nervous energy at first. While remaining calm and cool, channel that nervous energy into doing all the things you need to do to get ready to go to the hospital. These tasks include the following:

· Call the hospital to let them know what is going on.
· Call anyone – family member, doula – who may be assisting you in the labour.
· Make lunch and snacks for yourself (and snacks for your partner).
· Help your partner pack her stuff if she needs assistance (see page 172).
· Gather up what you need – toothbrush, birth aids, overnight bag, camera, camcorder.
· Pack the car, and don't forget the baby's car seat.

Take care of these things as soon as you can after your partner goes into early labour and her contractions become regular. With these tasks out of the way, you can better focus on assisting her. You will also have some peace of mind, knowing that when it is time to go to the hospital, you will be ready.

For a week or so before the due date, make sure that your car is always at least half-filled with petrol. For obvious reasons, you do not want to run out on the way to the hospital. It can't hurt to check the tyres, water and oil, either. Be sure everything is in good running order.

Be a Team Player

It is possible that while you're running around doing all these things to be helpful, your feelings may be hurt. Your partner may say something that doesn't seem appreciative of all that you have done and are doing for her. Later on, at the hospital, the nurses and doctors may ignore you as they focus their attention on her.

This is the way it goes when you're a birthing partner. It's not exactly a thankless job, because your partner appreciates what you're doing, although she may not be able to say so in the moment. Her family certainly appreciates you as well. But your needs, at this time, are secondary. Basically you've got to check your ego at the door and become a team player. In this case, that means serving your partner. Your job is to help her with whatever she needs in the moment. You will receive all the thanks you will ever need when you hold your baby in your arms.

The Best Place for Early Labour

In most first labours you will generally have time to assess the situation for a while before you have to take action.

You do not want to go to the hospital too early. If you arrive too soon and your partner's cervix is not adequately effaced and dilated, you will be sent back home. A high percentage of people having their first baby often make more than one trip to the hospital before giving birth. As disappointing as this can be, it is sometimes not such a bad thing. Home is a much better place to spend early labour.

Often what happens when you arrive at hospital, even if they admit you, is that your partner's contractions slow down. Although many hospitals have tried hard to make labour and delivery rooms more comfortable, they are still far less cozy than your own home. Whether she is conscious of doing this or not, your partner will probably tense up in this new unfamiliar environment. The tension she feels will then slow down her progress.

Keep in touch with the hospital. Tell them what is going on – the interval between your partner's contractions, whether or not her waters have broken, how long she has been labouring, how well she is coping. The midwives there will be your best guide.

The midwives are at the hospital. They cannot see your partner; they are relying on you to tell them what is going on. You and your partner are the best judge of what needs to be done at home. If you feel the situation warrants it, tell them you're coming in and want to be seen at the hospital.

The Drive to the Hospital

Driving your labouring partner to the hospital is one of the most important things you will do. It is anything but routine to be behind the wheel of a car while the person in the seat next to you is groaning with pain. You want to be attentive to her, and yet you have to keep your eyes on the road.

Here, again, cinema sets a bad example, in which the ride to the hospital is a high-speed dash involving jumping red lights and terrorizing pedestrians. This is probably not a wise approach.

Although you will naturally want to get to the hospital as quickly as you can, don't break the speed limit. Keep the ride smooth – a rough ride will only increase your partner's tension and pain, not ease it.

Very rarely, women in labour do give birth on the way to hospital. But these women are nearly always experiencing their second or third or fourth labours, not their first. If this is your first it is a good bet that, under normal circumstances, you will make it to the hospital in plenty of time.

Before you set off, make sure your partner has her seat belt on. The strap across her abdomen may be awkward and uncomfortable, but she still needs to put it on. If you have to brake suddenly or you're hit by somebody, she and your child need to be safe.

Studies have shown that accidents occur more frequently when people are distracted and have more than one thing on their mind. Stress can also cause people to try to handle too many things at once. When people narrow their focus and eliminate distractions, the accident rate decreases measurably.

The advice to drive safely may seem obvious and routine. But what sometimes happens to people in stressful situations is that they forget the obvious and act a little crazy. This includes fathers-to-be when they're driving their partners to the hospital.

It is exciting when labour finally starts for real. It is also a great relief. You have helped comfort your partner during early labour, taking walks with her, giving her the support she needs, timing her contractions, calling the hospital and informing the rest of the birth team. You have packed the car and are on your way to the hospital. The time is coming fast when you will finally meet your baby.

Chapter 16

Labour and Delivery

Helping deliver your child is unlike any experience you will ever have in your life. Your partner is going to work hard and endure incredible pain, and you are going to be with her the whole way. At the end, the two of you will have a baby. This chapter explains what you can expect and how to get through it.

Admission

The first thing you need to understand about having a baby is that although it may be a new experience for you and your partner, your local hospital or birth centre delivers babies all the time. It is anything but a novel experience for the hospital.

As such, you are going to be subject to certain routine admission procedures when you arrive with your partner. She may be suffering contractions and groaning with pain, but you may still have to produce her maternity notes and answer questions about the labour so far. They may not immediately rush your partner into the birthing room the way they do in films.

Childbirth preparation classes usually include a hospital tour. If you attended these classes, you probably already know the general layout of the hospital – where to park your car, where the maternity wing is, how to get there. It is important to check out things ahead of time because you really don't want to be wandering along the hospital corridors asking people for directions.

Patience is the rule when you check into the hospital. It may take time, much longer than you expect. You and your partner might sit in the room for a while. Staying relaxed and calm may help your partner do the same.

Once the midwives decide to admit your partner, she will be asked to undress and put on her nightdress. Her blood pressure, temperature, urine and pulse will be checked. Two monitoring belts may be wrapped around her belly with two gadgets: a transducer to measure the foetal heartbeat, and a monitor to gauge the strength and duration of her contractions. These measurements will be recorded on a display monitor and printed out on graph-like paper.

A midwife or doctor will give your partner a vaginal examination to determine how far her cervix is effaced and dilated. These terms are foreign to most men at first, but you will soon be an expert on them.

'Nothing Much Is Happening'

One of the most frustrating things that can happen is for a couple to arrive at the hospital thinking that the woman is about to give birth, and on examination to be told that 'nothing much is happening yet', Your partner may cry tears of disappointment if this happens. You may be advised that you might be better off at home. If you prefer to wait at the hospital, you will probably be sent to the antenatal ward.

Your partner's cervix must be dilated 10cm (4in) in order to begin the pushing that precedes birth. To be admitted into the hospital, either her waters should have broken or she must be in the neighbourhood of 4cm (1⅝in). If she is dilated less than this amount, her body is not yet close enough to giving birth.

It may feel like a real anticlimax going home, but this is sometimes the best thing. At home, your partner will feel more relaxed, and she may make more progress than if she had stayed at the hospital. Here are some things you can do if you are advised to return home:

· Let her express her disappointment at coming back home.
· Reassure her and encourage her that she is close to the 4cm mark and she will get there.
· Continue to walk gently with her to keep the labour moving along.
· Use your breathing techniques, the birth ball or other methods you have learned to help her manage the pain.
· Help her into the shower and let the hot water cascade off her back.
· Maintain a positive frame of mind, and keep encouraging her so she does the same.
· Drink water.
· Rest, rest, rest. (Both of you will need it.)

Rest for you both is vital, and yet you also want the labour to progress. Keep timing those contractions. You may have to go home for an hour or two, possibly spend the night, or be there for as long as a day. Keep in touch with the hospital. The midwives will advise you on when to come in again, based on the specifics of your situation.

Delivery Room Procedures

Once your partner reaches the magic threshold of 4cm or thereabouts, she will be admitted into a delivery room. Because you were generous enough to give up *Match of the Day* one evening and go down to the hospital to take the tour with your partner, you have already seen this room or one like it. It is the place where you will spend the next several hours until your baby is born.

As you walk down the hallway to your room, you may hear shouts emanating from behind the closed doors of other rooms. These are the cries of other labouring women. Pretty soon, however, you will hardly notice what is going on elsewhere in the wing. You will be focused on the incredible drama unfolding in your room.

Activity of Nurses

When you check into your delivery room, a midwife will be assigned to your partner. She will come in and talk to you both. She will have read the birth plan you brought with you and be familiar with your wishes for the birth.

She will ask your partner questions about the labour as well as her pregnancy history. She will want to know if she has had a show or if her waters are still intact. She may talk to you about pain medication. In most labour and delivery situations, you are going to interact more with the midwife than the consultant.

The midwife will be your main point of contact with the hospital staff, but that does not mean she will be spending every moment with you and your partner. She may have other labouring women to attend to. There may be one or more shift changes while you are there. The midwife you begin labour with may not be the same one you finish with.

Additionally, the midwife may only stay a few minutes when she checks up on you. She and her colleagues may pop in and out of your room.

Later, as the labour gains momentum and moves into the 'rock 'em, sock 'em' transition phase, the midwife will be a constant presence and a source of strength.

The Labour and Delivery Room

The centre of the labour and delivery room is your partner's bed. This is where she will be and where nearly all the action will take place. There will probably be a shower in your room. Some labour and delivery rooms also have birthing pools. The furnishings might include a large chair that folds into a bed, where you can sleep if the labour lasts overnight and you need to rest.

Your partner is probably still hooked up to the monitors strapped to her abdomen. In high-risk pregnancies, or when the baby is having problems, the doctor may also decide to connect her to an internal foetal monitor. In this procedure, an electrode is inserted via the vagina through the woman's cervix and clipped on the baby's scalp. This kind of monitoring supplies more precise measurements than external means.

In some cases, a woman needs an intravenous drip. This can be used to give a saline solution to replenish the fluids she is losing due to her extreme exertion. It can also be used to administer pain-killing drugs and oxytocin, a drug that induces or speeds labour along, if needed.

The Birth Team

Childbirth was traditionally seen as a female process, undertaken and supervised by women with little or no involvement from men. Nowadays, women are still the dominant players, but it is no longer their exclusive domain. Most births in the UK take place in hospital, with both male and female doctors and midwives participating. Then, of course, there's you, Dad, doing your bit as labour partner.

Ideally, having a baby is a team effort. You and your partner have a team to help you deliver your child. The goal of every member of the team is the same: a healthy and safe delivery for both mother and baby.

The Non-medical Team

Every birth team has two sides: the medical and the non-medical. As birth partner, your main job is to assist your partner in any way she needs it. You do what needs to be done, and you make decisions.

If you chose to recruit some help from a family member or a doula, this person is also part of the non-medical side of your team. She is there so that the entire burden of helping your partner does not fall on you.

The Medical Side

The medical side of your team consists of the midwife, the duty consultant or registrar, the anaesthetist and other medical aides who may assist during the birth. They are trained professionals. They have delivered babies countless times before, and you will rely on their expertise and experience to do it yet again.

As your partner's chief advocate and the father of the child, you have a voice in what goes on in the labour and delivery room. Ultimately, however, the medical staff are in charge. They have the final say on matters related to the health and safety of your partner and child.

Possible Friction Between the Sides

You may be saying to yourself, 'Well, of course, the doctors are going to have the final word, and thank God for that. I'm not trained to make medical decisions.' But it's slightly more complicated than that. When the issue is clear-cut – for example, if the baby is in extreme distress and an emergency caesarean section must be performed – the medical staff will act quickly and decisively (see Chapter 17).

Communication is vital during labour and delivery. Keep your partner posted on what you're doing. If you have to leave the room, remember to tell her before you go. If you have to leave the building to move the car or for any other reason, be sure to tell the midwife where you are and how soon you will be back.

In many normal labour and delivery situations, however, the right thing to do is not precisely clear in that moment. The midwife may offer pain medication to your partner. But she may not yet be emotionally ready to accept that. She may want to keep working and being in labour for a while longer to see if she can make more progress before using drugs.

Neither side – your partner's or the midwife's – is right or wrong; they're just different approaches. In the end, your partner may accept medication. In deciding what works for you, you may occasionally encounter some friction or a disagreement with the hospital staff. But remember that you're all on the same team, working to the same goal.

When Labour Stalls

To be admitted to the hospital in a normal delivery, your partner has to be dilated to 4cm (1⅝in) or thereabouts. But that is less than halfway up the mountain you need to climb. The two of you still have a lot of work to do. Her cervix needs to dilate 6cm (2⅜in) more and become 100 per cent effaced before your baby can be born.

It may take many hours to reach the 4cm mark. You may have driven to the hospital, been turned away and had to go back home. Finally, after many more arduous and painful contractions, you and your partner are admitted to the delivery room.

It is always possible, of course, that this next phase will go smoothly and that your partner will make solid, steady progress. It is also possible that the labour will slow down at some point. Your partner will continue having regular and frequent contractions, but they will not bring her any closer to that all-important 10cm (4in) mark.

Sometimes midwives do not pay as much attention to your partner as you would like. If your labour has stalled, you may need to find your midwife and request that she become more actively engaged. Her energy and knowledge may give you and your partner the boost you need.

For example, she could jump from 4cm to 6cm relatively quickly. Then an hour or so could pass, filled with hard contractions. Your midwife could then return and do another check but this time deliver the bad news that you're still at 6cm – no progress. It's discouraging.

What do you do then? Encourage your partner, help her shift into different positions to stimulate the labour. Get her up and walking, if she can. Give her ice cubes for thirst and make sure she is comfortable. Continue to use the breathing and other techniques you've learned, and keep plugging away.

Pain Relief Options

Labour and delivery is not an endurance contest. The point of it is not to see how much pain your partner can withstand. Pain medication is a valid and widely used option for women in labour.

For many men, it is difficult to see the women they love in so much pain. It is far more difficult, of course, for the woman to suffer through this pain. Drugs can provide relief for her.

Epidural

Many women who have had babies like to joke that the sexiest man they have ever met is the anaesthetist who gave them an epidural during labour. Before the anaesthetist entered the picture, these women were suffering hugely. After he left, they felt much, much better. Some women, it is said, even name their babies after their anaesthetists.

An epidural block, as it is formally called, is safe and easy to administer through an injection in the spine. One big reason that women like it – apart from the fact that it takes them out of pain – is that they can remain awake during labour. The pain relief extends to the lower part of the body, leaving the head clear. When the woman's child is born, she can welcome her with open arms and an alert mind.

Many couples decide in advance that they want to have an epidural and include it in their birth plans. Even so, this doesn't let them entirely off the hook. If your partner gets an epidural too early in the process, it can slow down her delivery. That means you both are going to have to work and labour for a while to reach the point at which the medication can achieve the best results.

Analgesics

Pethidine is another form of pain medication used in labour. It is usually administered as an injection, and is not only a painkiller but also helps the labouring woman to relax.

Pethidine is often combined with an anti-emetic (a drug to control sickness) because it can cause sickness. Remember that it takes about 15 minutes for the drug to kick in, so you'll both need to use those breathing techniques while you wait. This drug has been used safely for over 60 years, and many women say it helps a lot. Others, however, find it makes them feel weepy, sleepy and sick. It can slow labour down and, because it crosses the placenta and reaches your baby, he may need to have an injection as soon as he is born to reverse the effects of the drug in his newborn system.

Your partner cannot have pethidine if your midwife thinks she is close to giving birth because it would have a very adverse effect on the baby. Make sure she has a vaginal examination to see how far dilated she is before opting for pethidine. If she is further on than she thought, she may decide that she can manage without it after all.

If you and your partner originally wanted to do a 'natural' delivery, without the use of an epidural or other drugs, circumstances may evolve that force you to change your mind. Your partner may be in so much pain, and making so little progress, that you feel you have no other choice.

Before you make the final decision, however, give yourself some time to think about it. During that period, you might make enough progress that the drugs are no longer warranted. An epidural, however, can only be administered at a certain stage in labour, so you can't wait too long before you make this decision.

Pushing

Pushing may be the best time in all labour. Your partner has worked her way through early and active labour. She has survived the stormy stage known as transition, which has opened her cervix from about 7cm to 10cm (2¾in to 4in). Having arrived there, she can finally push. Being able to push her baby out, to exert herself in this way, often gives a woman a renewed sense of power and energy.

It's a good time for you, too. You've travelled this long road with her. You've been there the whole way, and the end appears to be in sight. Contrary to popular belief, however, pushing seldom ever takes only a few minutes. It can last anywhere from 30 minutes to two hours or longer.

With your partner pushing and becoming more physically assertive, her legs are spread wide and she may be back on her buttocks or kneeling on all fours. Both you and the midwife intently watch the monitor to see when the next contraction is coming on. She can push when a contraction comes on. She grits her teeth and summons all her energy while you encourage her and tell her to give it everything she has.

After the contraction passes, she relaxes. Then another contraction comes up and she makes another supreme effort. And another and another. During the contractions, her voice rises to a scream, but you tell her that her cries only disperse her energy. She needs to direct her power downwards with a low, guttural growl.

Down and out, that's your message to your partner. Down and out. Then your baby's head appears for the first time in the birth canal.

Congratulations! You're a Father!

By this time, the duty consultant may have arrived to watch the birth. The room may be a hive of activity. There may be several midwives and a paediatrician in the room, preparing sterile instruments in case they are needed and getting things ready for when the baby emerges. A mirror has been brought in so that your partner can see the baby, if she wishes.

The baby's head comes forwards, then back. Forwards, then back. This is called 'crowning'. More pushing is required, more straining, more grunting. Then comes one last push, and there he is.

First Impressions

You may fall rapturously in love with your child on first sight. Or you may take one look at your newborn and think 'Yuck!' His wrinkly skin may look discoloured. His head may be slightly misshapen. Both these conditions will go away with time. Your child's skin tones will gradually look the way they should. The 'conehead' effect, which is caused by his recent journey, snaking his way down the narrow birth canal, will also diminish, and his head will be an ordinary shape.

Cutting the Cord

Many men choose to cut their child's umbilical cord. This is a simple, safe and easy procedure. The cord is clamped off on either side by the medical staff, leaving you a small area to snip with a pair of scissors that they give you. Don't worry; you won't slip.

The act of cutting the cord has grown in popularity in recent years. It is another way in which men can be involved in the act of childbirth. There is a symbolic aspect to it. The father is the one who severs the physical connection between mother and child. If it is not something that appeals to you, however, all you have to do is say no, thank you.

Another recent trend in the USA is to store, or 'bank', your child's umbilical cord blood. Cord blood is a rich source of stem cells. If your child or family member developed cancer or a blood disease later in life, these stem cells could potentially be used in treatment.

Holding the Baby

Virtually all mothers are going to want to hold their babies and have skin-to-skin contact with them as soon after birth as possible. This is right and proper. Mum did all the work (or most of it); she gets first cuddle. Almost immediately, the midwife or your doula will help show her how to breastfeed her baby.

After Mum, though, it's your turn. Don't be shy; give it a whirl. Before they become fathers, lots of men are not quite sure about holding a baby. It's like a baby is some sort of rare and expensive antique vase. They fear they'll drop her or hold her wrong and somehow hurt her.

Once you become a father, these fears disappear. She's your daughter; of course you're going to pick her up and hold her. You've never met her before, and you're only starting to get to know her. But you have been through a lot together already, and you have formed a relationship. And your relationship is only beginning.

The Placenta

So the baby has entered the world. She's healthy, and you're bonding up a storm with her. OK, time to pack it up and go home, right? No, not quite. There is still another job to do: delivering the placenta.

The placenta, or afterbirth, has sustained your child while inside the womb, feeding and supporting her. Its job is done, and it cannot remain inside your partner's body. It has to come out. It emerges the same way the baby did: travelling down the birth canal.

Delivering the placenta can take anywhere from five to 25 minutes or more. Your partner will continue to have contractions (though milder than before), which means that you've got to help her get through them. Turn your attention back to your partner, encouraging her and helping her to finish this one last job. When she's done, you're done.

Be aware, too, that your partner may need to be stitched up after birth. The perineum is the skin on the bottom side of the vaginal opening. She may have had an episiotomy or incision to prevent bad tearing in this area, or she may have torn from the exertions of labour. This will be an uncomfortable several minutes for her.

And so you and your partner have made your journey. You checked into the hospital as a couple, and then, with the birth team assembled around your partner and working as a unit, the most amazing and mind-blowing event of your life occurred. Your baby was born. You will leave the hospital as a family.

Chapter 17

Real-Life Birth Scenarios

The Boy Scout motto of 'Be prepared!' is an excellent rule for expectant fathers, and mothers, too. But sometimes things happen when you're having a baby that you're not prepared for. In fact, you can almost count on it. This chapter tells you about some of the unexpected things that can happen and how to get ready for them.

Expect the Unexpected

Like most pregnant couples these days, you will write a birth plan explaining how you would like the labour and delivery to proceed – whether or not your partner wants to have an epidural or other pain medication, whether she wants to be connected to an IV drip or have electronic foetal monitoring during labour, what the atmosphere of the delivery room should be like, and so forth.

Many pregnant couples (particularly the mother-to-be) spend a great deal of time thinking about and writing their plan. Some are quite detailed and specific, with precise instructions to the medical staff on a number of issues related to the birth. No matter how detailed your plan is, however, you can never predict what will happen during your child's birth. Almost certainly, something is going to occur that you did not expect and did not plan for.

This does not necessarily mean that what will happen will be bad, although, unfortunately, sometimes bad things do happen during childbirth. What it means is that it will be different, a variation from the birth plan you so carefully laid out. You have to be prepared for being unprepared, for the possibility that an unexpected turn of events will catch you off guard.

Flexibility Is the Key

How do you prepare for the unexpected? You do all the things you're doing now: you read about pregnancy, talk to your partner, talk to other people who have had children, go to antenatal classes. While none of this will specifically instruct you on how to handle an abrupt change in plans, it will give you a solid grasp of what occurs during labour and delivery. This general understanding will help you deal with whatever comes up.

You will need to be flexible. So will your partner. Although you may have put a lot of time and care into your birth plan, it is not a tablet carved in stone. You will be better off if you approach labour and delivery with the idea that unexpected events can occur, and that these events may cause you to change your plans.

Talk about contingency plans with your partner and work out some 'What will we do if' scenarios. She may have strong ideas about the birth and be unwilling to talk about alternatives. Support what she wants, but gently try to come up with a Plan B and even a Plan C. You may not need to use these backup plans, but it is good to be prepared.

Premature Birth

A full-term pregnancy is defined as one that reaches anywhere from the 37-week mark to 42 weeks. A birth is premature when the baby is born earlier than 37 weeks. If you are expecting twins, there is a high probability that your bundles of joy will arrive before 37 weeks. This means that you and your partner need to have everything in place and be ready to go to the hospital at least a couple of weeks before then.

No one can say precisely what causes many babies to be born prematurely. But medical experts have been able to pinpoint certain risk factors for premature birth. In addition to having twins or a multiple birth, those factors include the following:

- Drug use (cannabis, ecstasy, cocaine)
- Poverty
- Vaginal or urinary tract infection
- Previous premature birth
- Previous abortion or late miscarriage
- Smoking
- Domestic violence
- Cervical abnormality

Take It Seriously

Premature labour can be a very serious threat and needs to be treated as such. It is the leading cause of neonatal death. Premature babies who survive sometimes have health problems that last throughout their lives. If your partner goes into early labour, she needs immediate medical attention. Phone the hospital, even if it's the middle of the night.

Depending on the pregnancy, however, having early labour contractions does not necessarily mean that your partner is immediately going to give birth. Doctors sometimes tell pregnant women to go to bed and stay there as a means of preventing or delaying labour. Mothers-to-be may need to stop working or cease physical activities (including sexual intercourse). In some cases, doctors may recommend special medication or hospitalization. This is all because it is better for the baby to stay inside her mother until she reaches full term, or as close as possible.

Although it is more likely that your partner will be late in delivering than it is that she'll be early, you need to consider this possibility in your planning. If your partner has to leave her job early, this could affect your financial situation.

In the United Kingdom, between 6 and 7 per cent of babies are born prematurely, according to figures from the Department of Health.

Furthermore, if the doctor orders partial or complete bed rest for her, you may have to do more around the house than you originally reckoned on doing. Her family and friends may also have to get more involved earlier than expected. Yours, too. Everybody may need to pitch in to help bring this baby to term.

Emergency Roadside Delivery

It's a scenario straight out of a film. A woman is in labour, and her husband is frantically driving her to the hospital. 'No, no', she tells him between groans. 'We're not going to make it. The baby is coming... now!' Panicked out of his mind, the husband whips their car over to the side of the road and jumps out. Quickly he runs around to the passenger door in time to see his baby's head emerging from between his wife's legs.

An ambulance and police car arrive a moment later, but by then the deed is done. Dad has delivered the baby, safe and sound, on the side of the road miles before they reached the hospital. The next day the new family poses for a picture in the local paper.

Curiously enough, this improbable scenario does actually occur in real life. Every now and then, women in labour do not make it all the way to the hospital, giving birth on the side of the road. Sometimes women give birth at home, before they've even managed to get into the car to head for the hospital.

Fortunately, if this is your partner's first labour and delivery, you need not worry too much about this. Emergency roadside deliveries are extremely rare. And when they do happen, it's almost always to women who are having their second child, labours that usually proceed much more quickly than first births. So you've got time – time enough, at any rate, to drive safely.

Medical Intervention

'Normal' is a term that is often used in connection with pregnancy. The expressions 'under normal circumstances' and 'with normal births' are common and have been used frequently in this book. It is reassuring for expectant parents to know that the pregnancy is proceeding as it should and that their unborn child is developing normally.

This applies to labour and delivery as well. Parents want their child's birth to proceed normally, but there is a wide variation in what this means. One couple's 'normal' may be completely different from another's. Many things can happen during labour and delivery. Some cases may require medical intervention, such as the following:

· The woman may have back labour, causing her intense pain.
· The baby may be in a 'breech' position, with his buttocks rather than his head coming first down the birth canal.
· The baby isn't making any progress, requiring doctors to use forceps or ventouse (suction) to guide the baby out of the birth canal.

- The umbilical cord can get wrapped around the baby's neck, which may restrict blood flow.
- The cord can become compressed, reducing or perhaps cutting off the flow of oxygen.
- The baby may have had his first bowel movement in the womb, causing a darkish staining (meconium).
- The baby could be listless after birth, perhaps due to pain medication given to the mother.

Results are what count in the labour and delivery business. These and many other things can happen. Some may require immediate treatment by the midwives and doctors. Just know that you can have a wild, wild birth and still end up with a healthy, happy, normal baby.

Forceps were invented by a 16th-century British physician named Peter Chamberlen the elder, though the instrument didn't come into common use until the late 1800s. These tong-like instruments, used far less commonly today than in the past, have curved ends that cradle the baby's head. The doctor then pulls gently as your partner has a contraction in order to move her down the birth canal.

Baby Is Late

You can practically take a bet on this one. If this is your partner's first baby, and everything is 'normal', the child will very probably be born later than its due date. This can be a very frustrating time. You've had the due date circled on your calendar for months and months. Finally, the big day arrives – and what happens? Nothing. After all that waiting, the only thing you and your partner can do is to wait a bit longer.

This can be a tough time for both of you. First of all, you've had your expectations dashed. Although you knew that most first births arrived late, somehow you hoped that yours would be different.

Another frustrated group is your family and friends. Even if you wisely did not reveal the exact due date, telling them only approximately when the birth would occur, they know the general timetable and are starting to e-mail and phone you and your partner more frequently. This only adds to the pressure you're feeling.

Your First Lesson in Parenting

If your baby is overdue, this is actually your first lesson in parenting. You may have a timetable for your child and a certain set of expectations for her. But that does not mean she is going to follow the timetable you've laid out for her or any of your expectations. What's true for teenagers and other children goes for babies just as well. They have their own agenda.

Nevertheless, you can do your best to keep things moving along. It is said that stimulating a woman's nipples may lead to contractions, but only if you do it for long hours at a time. Sexual intercourse is another fun activity to try. After the two of you are finished in bed, you might take a gentle walk together around the block. Walking may help stir things up for her as well.

Other home remedies for stimulating labour include raspberry-leaf tea or evening primrose oil. None of these techniques should be attempted, however, without first asking your midwife. Depending on how 'late' you baby is, your doctor may recommend oxytocin as a means of inducing the labour. But the best thing to do may be nothing at all – just let nature take its course.

Generally, obstetricians do not like pregnant women to go beyond the 42-week mark, or two weeks past the due date. The placenta may begin to deteriorate at this point. Most, though not all, women are induced at that point to go into labour.

Caesarean Delivery

The caesarean section was named after Julius Caesar who, it was said, was born via this surgical procedure. Historians scoff at this claim, however, because in the days of the ancient Roman Empire, using surgery to deliver a child was nearly certain to result in the death of the mother, and Julius's mother lived to a ripe old age. Nevertheless, the name stuck.

A caesarean section is a surgical procedure used to deliver babies. It is a common procedure and is considered relatively safe, although it still poses higher risks to the mother than a vaginal delivery. Although the health risks are minor, it is nevertheless regarded as major surgery.

Caesareans are performed for a variety of reasons. The mother's pregnancy may be high-risk, and a caesarean may be the safest way to deliver the baby. Delivering vaginally may pose problems, causing distress for the baby. The physicians may decide to get him out as quickly as possible, through surgical means. Some, though not all, doctors routinely perform caesareans when the baby is breech – pointing his bottom, not his head, down the birth canal.

Unless your partner's pregnancy is considered high-risk, and she knows from the start that there is a strong likelihood of a caesarean, she is probably not planning for one. Nearly all of the women who have had a caesarean originally thought they were going to deliver vaginally. But circumstances can change during the course of pregnancy or labour, and it is a good idea to know a bit about them, should your partner's situation warrant it.

Being a Birth Partner at a Caesarean Birth

Just as few women start out their pregnancies thinking about having a caesarean, few men consider the possibility that they may be comforting their partners not in the delivery room, but in the operating theatre. So the first thing is that the two of you need to at least entertain the possibility that it could happen. Have a 'What if?' sort of discussion. Talk about how you want to handle a caesarean, if it should occur, and then put those thoughts down in your birth plan.

A caesarean is a surgical procedure, and you and your partner will have less of a voice in what goes on in the operating theatre than if she were going through a vaginal delivery. Nevertheless, you can state your wishes. Does your partner want to hold the baby after surgery and perhaps even try to breastfeed her while she is still on the operating table? If you've thought about these things ahead of time, and written them down in a birth plan, you will not be caught off guard should your doctor tell you that a caesarean is necessary.

Your Place Is in the Operating Room

Only in rare cases are fathers not allowed to be with their partners in the operating room during a caesarean. This is likely to be in an emergency or when general anaesthesia is used and the mother is unconscious.

The decision to have a cesarean is sometimes made in the heat of the moment by doctors who need to extricate the baby, for the safety of both mother and baby. In an emergency, if you are excluded from the operating room, you will obviously not have time to discuss the decision. You may feel some disappointment in not being able to participate in the birth of your child.

It is generally agreed that many caesareans are unnecessary. Find out what the caesarean rate is at your hospital. If the percentage seems too high (over 25 per cent), you and your partner may want to look into having her give birth in another hospital. Some doctors may be too quick to resort to a caesarean during a slow or more difficult labour.

Your Job in the Room

Since this is surgery, you will scrub your hands and arms and wear sterile hospital clothes. In the operating room, you will sit at your partner's head behind a screen which blocks your view of the surgery that is taking place on the lower half of your partner's body. She will receive anaesthesia, which will numb her body but keep her conscious. You can hold her hand and talk to her while the surgery is taking place.

Even though a caesarean is safe, your partner will almost certainly feel anxious and scared. She may be scared, not so much for herself but for her child, whom she cannot see. She cannot feel the lower part of her body, and she has lost control over the birth of the baby, which is now in the hands of the surgeons. Stroke your partner's forehead and softly reassure her.

When the Baby Is Born

Next comes the best news of all. After just a few minutes, your child is born. Your partner will want to hold the baby as soon as possible, and, as labour partner, you should make sure she gets that opportunity. Because this is a surgical procedure, nurses and doctors follow a certain routine. Sometimes they can focus on this routine to such an extent that they overlook the urgent desire of the parents to connect with their newborn. Both you and your partner can hold the baby. If it's allowed, she may wish to try breastfeeding.

Some hospitals try to give the parents of caesarean babies more of an intimate post-birth family experience, instead of whisking the child away immediately to the neonatal intensive care unit. But it cannot compare to the time that parents have after a vaginal delivery. The mother in a caesarean birth has just undergone major surgery, and she must have her abdomen stitched up.

Go with Your Child

Your duty, at this point, is to hold your child while the surgeons look after your partner. If your baby is small or unwell, she may need to go to the special care baby unit. You can go with her. You can talk to her and sing to her, and tell her how much you love her. Let her wrap her tiny fingers around one of yours.

Once your partner is released from recovery and given a room in the maternity ward, she will be reunited with the baby and you.

Recovery from a Caesarean

Recovering from a caesarean section is generally longer and more painful than a vaginal delivery. Not only is your partner recovering from childbirth, she has just had major surgery. Anticipate, then, that she will be facing some big physical and emotional issues in the days and weeks to come.

Physically, it is going to be hard for her to get around at first. Immediately after birth, for example, she cannot lift up the baby. The child needs to be handed to her. She will feel a certain degree of pain, although medication will ease this. After you come home, she will be on extremely limited duty. You may need to enlist recruits – family members, a paid aide – to help you out around the house.

As she recovers physically, you need to be aware that there may be emotional fallout from the caesarean. This was not how she imagined childbirth. She may have gripes about the consultants, feeling that they ignored her during the surgery and should have been more attentive to her feelings. She may resent the fact that she did not get to hold her newborn as much as she liked, or that you had a better chance to bond with the baby straight after birth.

Back in the 1950s, fewer than 3 per cent of women in the UK had their babies by Caesarean section. But figures have risen dramatically. During the 1980s, 10 per cent of deliveries were by Caesarean section; by the mid-1990s the figure had climbed to 15 per cent; and today a staggering one in five births in the UK are Caesareans.

If your partner feels this sort of resentment, all you can do is let her talk and then show her some sympathy. You do not want her feelings to fester. You want her to talk about them so she can let go and move ahead with her life. The birth may not have been everything she dreamed of, but you have a vibrant, healthy child, and that is what matters most of all.

Trusting Your Instincts (and Hers)

This chapter has discussed various, real-life birth scenarios. However, a full discussion of all the things that could happen to you and your partner during labour and delivery would require far more than a single chapter. You could fill several books and still not cover every conceivable situation that could occur.

So what do you do? How do you prepare for all these potential scenarios? In the end, you have to trust your instincts. When faced with a decision, after discussing and exploring the various options, you are going to have to go with your gut feelings.

Equally important – perhaps even more important – is trusting your partner's instincts. That doesn't mean that she (or you) is always going to be right. But she is locked into that baby, and if she has a strong feeling about something, you need to listen to it, and probably follow her lead.

When you are having a baby, expect the unexpected. But if you trust your instincts and your partner's instincts, you will be ready for anything that comes your way.

Chapter 18

The Immediate Aftermath

Congratulations! You did it! You're a father. But your job isn't over yet. In some ways, in fact, it's only beginning. Before you can bring your partner and child home, you still have some work to do. This chapter explores the various things that come up immediately after the baby is born.

Taking a Moment with Your New Family

First things first. Before you make any calls to let people know; before the relatives and friends descend on the hospital; before all the craziness associated with having a baby begins, take a moment with just the three of you. You, your partner, your child – alone together for the first time. Isn't life grand?

At the moment of birth, the labour and delivery room was a frenzy of activity. Your partner was straining and pushing while you cheered her on. Then the baby was born, and shortly thereafter the midwife gave him to your partner so she could hold him and begin to learn how to breastfeed. Amidst all this, you snipped the umbilical cord and got to hold the baby yourself for the first time.

But at some appropriate moment, you and your new family have a right to some peace and quiet. Ask the medical staff, the doula and anyone else who may have assisted in the labour to leave the room because you and your partner want to be alone with the baby. It's not rude at all, and everyone will understand.

There is an understandably anxious feeling that comes with being left alone with a newborn for the first time. If you and your partner do not feel comfortable, ask a midwife to stay in your room for a few minutes. As your confidence grows, she can leave. Ask her to look in on you again in ten minutes.

Baby Health Checks

Certain medical tests and procedures will be performed on your baby in the delivery room or later. They will be done quickly and unobtrusively, immediately after birth or shortly thereafter. The tests measure your child's health and check that his bodily systems are firing on all cylinders.

The first test your child will receive is the Apgar. This is an acronym for the categories that the test scores: appearance, pulse, grimace (reflex) and respiration. The Apgar is administered twice – the first time at one minute after birth, and the second time at five minutes after. The child receives scores in each of the four categories, with most babies receiving a passing mark of seven to ten. Here are some other tests and procedures that the medical staff may administer:

- Suction nose to clear air passages.
- Clamp umbilical cord (after you cut it).
- Weigh and measure baby.
- Visually inspect baby, and count fingers and toes.
- Measure circumference of head.
- Apply eye drops or ointment to prevent infection.
- Give vitamin K injection to promote blood clotting.
- Draw blood from baby's heel for disease screening.
- Perform other types of blood screenings.

Some of these tests, such as the administration of vitamin K, either by injection or orally, and the heel prick, do not need to be administered immediately. Another routine but essential part of a hospital birth is having identification bracelets placed on your baby's wrist and ankle, your partner and possibly even on you. Everyone wants to be sure that you take the right child home with you.

Letting Everyone Know

It is definitely Dad's job to make the calls to tell people that the baby is here and Mum is doing fine. Mum will be able to receive calls and chat on the phone once she feels rested enough to talk. But Dad is the one who usually makes the first calls to family and friends.

Not every assignment you have as a father and birth partner is fun, but this one is. After the focused intensity of the labour and delivery experience, you get to reconnect with the outside world. By this time, although you will be tired and perhaps a little punch-drunk, you will be riding an emotional high. Your emotions will be shared by those on the other end of the line, who will be eager to hear every morsel of information you can give them.

Two Common Questions

People mainly have two questions at first. They want to know how Mum is doing, and they want to know whether it's a boy or a girl. If you have kept the name of your child a secret, this will be your first chance to break the news. Some people will want to know when they can talk to Mum, and they may even ask how you are holding up.

The average weight of a newborn is 3.4kg (7½lb), with nearly all babies tipping the scales between 2.5 and 4.5kg (5½ and 10lb). A newborn can lose as much as 10 per cent of his body weight in his first day or two of life. The average length of a newborn is 51cm (20in), with most measuring somewhere between 46 and 56cm (18 and 22in).

When the time finally comes to make these calls, you may have been up all night. You may not be thinking all that clearly. Therefore it is a good idea to make a list ahead of time of the people you need to call immediately: parents (hers and yours), family members (hers and yours) and close friends. You do not want to forget anyone important.

Mobile Phones

As discussed earlier in this book, a mobile phone is probably a good idea if you do not mind leaving the building. Most hospitals do not allow the use of mobiles, so bring lots of change with you in order to make calls from the hospital pay phone. Many hospital pay phones are on a wheeled trolley that can be brought into the room.

If you need to leave the room to make calls, or for any other reason, check with your partner first. This could be the first time she has ever been left alone with the baby. Be sure she is comfortable and taken care of before you go.

When to Call People

Some people, usually family members who are close to Mum, will say to you, 'Phone me as soon as you know. I don't care if it's three o'clock in the morning. I want to know the instant the baby is born!'

In almost every case, these calls can wait until a decent hour of the morning. Do not feel obliged to make calls in the middle of the night. Wait until the morning instead. The same people who are begging for you to call will appreciate the fact that you've allowed them to get a full night's sleep, whether they admit it or not. If they give you any grief for not calling them earlier, tell them you were distracted and exhausted, which, almost certainly, will be true.

Other Jobs and Responsibilities

Your first responsibilities are to your partner and child. Everything else is a distant third. If you keep this in mind, you will have no trouble working out what needs to be done, and in what order, after the birth takes place.

Once the baby is born, the big work is done (at least while the mother and child are still in the hospital). You and your partner have successfully completed your mission, and you can relax. But, in addition to phoning friends and relatives, there are some jobs you may be called upon to perform.

Being with the Baby

You may immediately need to start looking out for the welfare of your child, even while she is still in the hospital. In a caesarean birth, for example, the nurses may take the baby from the operating theatre after surgery is over. The father's responsibility is to go with his child and be with her while Mum remains behind in the doctors' hands.

In certain situations there may be fears about the child's health, and medical tests are conducted on these babies after birth. These tests are more sophisticated than the health tests carried out in the labour and delivery room, and they may take place in the neonatal intensive care unit.

In these cases, if possible, the father should accompany the baby while Mum recovers in her room.

Gatekeeper

Your partner will naturally be excited after the birth. But she will also be exhausted. Lots of people are going to call and want to talk to her. Still more people are going to want to visit.

One of your biggest jobs will be as gatekeeper. Obviously, you do not want to act like a bouncer at a nightclub. Just check with your partner now and then to make sure she is handling everything well. She won't get the rest she needs if she's entertaining visitors one after the other.

Breastfeeding Support

Breastfeeding (discussed more extensively in Chapter 19) usually begins shortly after birth. The midwife (or doula) places the baby on Mom's breast and begins to teach her how to do it. Despite what many men think, women do not instinctively know how to breastfeed. This can be a very difficult and painful process to learn.

You and your partner have probably already discussed breastfeeding. If she plans to do it (and most women do, at least initially), your encouragement and support can play a useful role in helping her to get started. And you will need to show that support from day one.

The benefits of breast milk for babies are indisputable. It supplies more than 100 vitamins and nutrients that are not found in infant formula. Studies have shown that children who are breastfed tend to have higher IQs than those who are not. This is partly because of the nutrition these babies receive, but it is also because of the close interaction between mother and child, which encourages subsequent brain development.

Meeting Siblings

If you have a young child, some of this information may be familiar to you because you went through it not that long ago. The age of your child (or children) will determine how you handle the news of a baby on the way. Whatever your child's age, she deserves to know about the pregnancy at a relatively early stage. She will have questions and concerns, and you need to deal with them in a thoughtful way.

Anticipate that your child's concerns will be self-centred. Her focus will be on how the baby is going to affect her. A teenager may fret about having to share her room with a new brother or sister, or not being able to spend as much time with her friends. Younger children may worry that the baby is going to replace them in your affection, and that you won't have as much time to spend with them. There are numerous children's books that deal with sibling issues. Reading stories together may reassure your child and help her better understand what's coming.

At the hospital, when a sibling comes to meet the baby for the first time, it is nice to have them exchange gifts. The older sibling brings a small gift for the baby, who returns the favour – thanks to your foresight in buying something beforehand for the older child and stashing it in the bag you brought to the hospital.

Younger children need a lot of leeway. They haven't seen mummy for a couple of days, and they may be anxious about her. They will want to climb in bed with her and their new brother or sister, creating an ideal photo opportunity for you.

Taking Pictures

During the birth, you are going to have your hands full. You probably will not be able to stop to take pictures. Even if you do find a spare moment or two, sticking a camera in your partner's face and telling her to 'Smile!' while she is in the midst of a contraction will probably not be met with a warm reception.

After the birth, however, it's a different story. Get your camera out of your rucksack or overnight bag and hand it to a nurse. Ask her to take a picture of your new family – Mum, Dad, baby – posed together on the hospital bed in the hour after the birth.

Especially in the hospital, when Mum may not be able to get out of bed easily and is frequently holding the baby, Dad is the main photographer. There's nothing wrong with this; just remember to hand the camera to someone else now and then and get yourself into a picture or two. In many ways, the shots you take in the hospital will be among the most memorable you will ever have of your child. Those are the first hours and days of her life.

Other people will bring cameras to take pictures – the more the merrier. If you're using a digital camera, you can send photos of your child via e-mail or post them on a website, allowing friends, colleagues and distant relatives a chance to see the new arrival right away.

For a classic look, try using black-and-white film for some of your shots in the hospital. Besides the timeless feel it will give your photos, black-and-white film helps you avoid the yellow or green colour casts that are typical in photos shot under incandescent or fluorescent lighting.

Shooting with a Camcorder

If you have a digital or video camcorder, creating a video is a wonderful thing to do as well. One advantage of moving pictures is that you are able to record sounds – the first cries and gurgles of your child as well as the laughter and chatter of the family members who come to visit.

Using a camcorder during the birth, however, is somewhat more problematic. You may think it's a really good idea, but your partner may be dead set against it – and you must be prepared to respect her decision here. Before you go too far with your discussions, check with the hospital to see what its policy is. Some do not allow camcorders to be used during labour and delivery.

Shooting During Birth

The best technique is to set the camcorder up on a tripod in a spot in the room that gives you a view of the bed but that is not in anyone's way. Midwives and doctors come and go during labour and delivery. This activity increases in the moments before birth. The medical people cannot be bumping into the tripod while they're trying to deliver your baby.

Another reason for a tripod is that you need to have your hands free to help your partner. There may be moments where you can walk over to the camcorder and shoot some action. This will be much easier to do if it is already set up and ready to go than if you have to fumble around with it each time you want to use it.

During the all-out intensity of transition and pushing, as well as the quieter, more sublime moments right after birth, you cannot adequately do your job as birth partner while doubling as director of photography. You need to concentrate on your partner and the business at hand. You may solve this problem by bringing in a friend to handle the video or digital responsibilities.

Your Partner's Qualms

Your partner may be agreeable to the idea of videotaping the birth. Then again, she may have a single-spaced, five-page list of objections on why she is not going to allow this to happen. Listen to what she has to say. For one, she may not want these moments to be saved for posterity. Her body will be on view in a most revealing way. Furthermore, her face will be contorted with pain, she will cry and scream, she will sweat and groan and curse – not the kind of show you hire on Friday night at the video store.

And what about this mate of yours who is going to help with the filming? She may not want him in the room. She may only want those who are assisting in the birth to be present. She may worry – and there may be some justification for this – that you are going to be distracted by the filming and not be able to give her your full attention. On this issue, your partner deserves veto power. If she doesn't want to be filmed during birth, that's her decision to make. But remember to bring the camcorder with you. Nobody will object to filming after birth.

Celebrating the Arrival

Having a baby is a thing to celebrate. It's a unique moment in your life, and you and your partner have worked hard to reach it. With your family and closest friends around you, you deserve a good time. Relish the moment while you can.

Champagne is always good. Ask a friend to bring a bottle and some plastic glasses when he comes. Another way is flowers, which are usually on sale in the hospital gift shop.

A Gift for Mummy

No one is more deserving of something special than your partner. As you will see after you go through the birth with her, this woman gave her all to bring a child of yours into the world. It is the very least you can do to recognize this in some way.

You do not need to go into serious debt to buy diamond earrings or an expensive gift at this time. If you can swing it financially, that's great. But something simple and thoughtful – flowers and a card, for example – will do just fine.

You have, after all, given quite a bit of yourself as well. You've been with your partner the whole way, and now you have this beautiful, amazing, incredible baby. You were there when she needed you the most, and although it sounds corny, this was the greatest gift you could give her.

Taking Mother and Baby Home

Most maternity units now encourage 'rooming in', which means that mum keeps the baby with her at all times while the two are in the hospital, even when she goes to the loo or for a bath. The advantage of rooming in is that Mum always gets to be with her child, holding and cuddling and breastfeeding her. It is also much safer for the baby always to be in her mother's sight.

Your partner's rooming in with the baby will not affect you because you are not going to spend the night with them. You need to go home and get a good night's sleep. You will have plenty of nights in the future to share with your child and her mother. After you have rested, showered and had a couple of square meals, you can return to the hospital the next day to take them home.

Two-day stays in the hospital are generally recommended. Hospitals have been criticized in recent years for trying to discharge new mothers and babies after only a few hours or one day. If your partner feels ready and able to leave the hospital, and consultant and paediatrician consent, then take her home.

If you haven't done it already, install the child safety seat in your car. Hospital authorities are not supposed to release children unless the parents have a safety seat in their car. It is not safe for your partner to hold the baby in her arms while travelling in a moving vehicle. You could stop suddenly or be in an accident, and the child could be in danger.

The actor and comedian Will Smith has a funny bit about driving like a madman to the hospital on the night his wife delivers their baby. But afterwards, when he takes his baby home with him for the first time, he obeys all the traffic laws to the letter and drives as slowly and safely as he can. Not only that, he's yelling out of his window at all the crazy drivers on the road who pose a potential threat to his child. It's all a matter of perspective.

And how your perspective has changed! You finally started to understand what this fatherhood thing was all about when you took a moment with your new family after the baby was born. Now you begin the next phase of this wonderful but terrifying adventure.

Chapter 19

Baby Comes Home

When you bought a pram, assembled the crib, painted the nursery and prepared your house, you were getting ready for this very day – the day you get to bring your child home. But, having done all this, you will quickly discover that you are not prepared at all. This chapter describes how to cope with the arrival of baby and the chaotic times that are sure to follow.

So What Do We Do Now?

All new parents go through some version of an experience that goes something like this. They've endured nine or so months of pregnancy and a long labour – followed by a satisfying delivery – and finally they bring their baby home with them for the first time. The baby is sleeping, and it is quiet. The parents sit down on the couch together. One of them (often the man) looks at the other and says, 'So now what do we do?'

It is indeed a rather humbling thought. You've come so far, travelled all this way, and you really don't know the first thing about bringing up a child. You turn to your partner, expecting her to know the answer. But she just shrugs. She's never had a baby before, so how is she supposed to know what to do?

Because babies do not talk, it is often difficult to work out what they want. What they do, however, is not such a mystery. Babies do five basic things:

- Pee
- Poo
- Cry
- Eat
- Sleep

They can and will do two or more of these things at the same time. They frequently do these things (all but sleep, probably) in the middle of the night, and they may do them several times in the same night. Babies are peeing, pooing, crying, eating and sleeping machines. And they also puke up occasionally.

Introducing Baby to Your Pet

When you bring your baby home for the first time, your furry creature in residence may cosy up to you like a long-lost friend, wondering wordlessly where you have been and why you were away for so long. You can tell from its actions that it is glad to see you. You can also tell that it may be suspicious, to put it mildly, or not too keen at all about this strange new arrival in the house.

Both dogs and cats can come to feel that they own the house they live in. And why not? They have the run of the place. People let them in and out whenever they wish. These same people feed them and brush them and give them treats. Some animals are even accustomed to sleeping in their owners' beds.

Given all this, it is no wonder that your pet may look askance at a baby in the house. It may view the child as a potential rival or usurper. This is accurate. Your cat or dog has, in fact, been replaced as the ruler of the house. But it may be too much of a shock to his system to break this news to him immediately. Let him find out gradually, over a period of time.

Cats

A cat may feel particularly bent out of shape with the arrival of baby. Inevitably, his lap time with Mum and Dad will be severely reduced. In the past, he may have been able to wander freely about the house. This also has changed.

Keep the cat out of the baby's room. The easiest and most effective way to do this is to keep the door of the room shut while the baby is sleeping or resting in the crib. Some people put netting over the crib to keep the cat out of it. Get your cat to sleep in a large cat carrier if you do not want to close the baby's door.

An old piece of folklore says that cats suck the life out of babies. This tale probably came about when people noticed a cat licking drool from the corner of a baby's mouth. A baby drinks a lot of milk. Her breath and lips smell of milk. The smell of milk may be one reason why cats, who are naturally curious anyway, approached the baby when no one was looking.

Dogs

Descended from wolves, domesticated dogs are pack animals. Slowly introduce the newest member of your pack to your dog. Let him sniff an article of the baby's clothing after you come home. Dogs have incredible olfactory powers and can pick up a human scent even after the clothing has been washed and dried.

Better still, when Mum and baby are at the hospital, take a piece of clothing that your child has already worn. Bring it home, and let the dog have a sniff. This way, when baby makes her grand appearance, her scent will already be familiar to your dog, and in a short time the familiarity will allow the dog to be comfortable with the baby.

Never leave your cat or dog alone in a room with the baby. Nor is it a good idea to put a baby on a blanket with an animal nearby. Even if you are careful, you can never be sure what an animal is going to do. A cat, for example, may want to lie on the blanket too, swiping with its paw if it does not get what it wants.

Supporting Your Family

If you found a way to arrange it with work and to deal with it financially, you may be getting ready to spend a week or two with your partner and child. While you may not be at work during this time, make no mistake about it. This is no holiday. Baby is going to run you ragged.

If you were not able to get some time off after the baby was born, and you have to go back to work immediately, you will, in effect, have two jobs – the one that pays, and the one that doesn't. Your second, non-paying job will begin as soon as you get home from your paying one.

When you open the door, it may feel as if a hurricane hit you. Baby may be screaming and crying, and your partner may be going crazy. Your partner, who may have idealized what it was like to be a mum and stay at home with her newborn, has quickly come to realize what a tough, largely thankless, virtually non-stop job it is. She needs a break, and your main job will be to give it to her.

If you have stayed home with your partner to help her take care of the baby, you may be secretly relieved to go back to your job – the paying one. Not only are you glad to be earning money again, but you're also thrilled at the chance to get some time away from the craziness at home. Indeed, some men feel guilty about leaving their partners to handle the baby while they drive away each morning to work.

But it is useful to remember that the reason fathers work is to support their family. They are working for their families, even though they are not in the house. Nowadays, however, more is expected of men than to just supply a pay cheque. Be prepared to pitch in and do your share at home. This is another way you can support your family.

Being involved with your children pays off for them as babies and when they are older. Studies have shown that children with involved fathers performed better in school. These children also tend to be socially better adjusted and are far less likely to use drugs and commit crimes.

The Breastfeeding Challenge

Some men think that women instinctively know how to handle babies. This is not true, of course. Gender alone does not make her an instant expert. She has to learn all this stuff the same way you do – the hard way.

If you need proof of this, wait till she begins to breastfeed the baby. This process may sound easy and even automatic at first – although it is anything but that.

You're Involved, Like It or Not

Being a man, your first thought may be, 'Well OK, so breastfeeding may be a little tough on her. What does that have to do with me?' In a word, plenty. If she is miserable because the breastfeeding is going so poorly, and if the baby is losing weight because he's not getting enough food, that is going to affect you. You are going to be drawn into the middle of this, like it or not.

Her first attempts at breastfeeding will begin in the hospital. So will your first expressions of support for her. But that is not the end of it, not by a long shot. If you want your partner to breastfeed – and there are many sound health reasons why breast milk is superior to formula – you will need to continue to offer support, through your words and deeds.

A Blow to Their Femininity

For many new mothers, breastfeeding is wrapped up in their sense of themselves as women. Many women expect to breastfeed and eagerly look forward to it. There is something innately female about nursing. Only women can produce milk out of their breasts, from which they can supply food and nourishment to their offspring.

When a new mother encounters difficulties in breastfeeding her baby – and many do – it is sometimes seen as a blow to her femininity. Is there something wrong with her as a woman, as a mother? Your partner may torture herself with questions of this nature. If so, you may see tears of frustration from her.

In addition, your partner will almost certainly experience physical discomfort from breastfeeding, especially at the beginning, when she and the baby are still getting their act together. Her nipples may become chapped and raw.

Getting Some Help

Possibly adding to your partner's woes is her concern for her child. Nearly all babies lose a little weight after they come home from the hospital and before they gradually start putting on weight. But your child may not be gaining as much as you think she should. This may throw your partner into a panic and give her more guilt pangs because she fears she is starving her child.

When you only weigh a few kilos to begin with and you're only three or four days old, any weight loss can be a serious business. As with all things having to do with newborns, you need to stay in close touch with your midwife or health visitor about your baby's weight. Ask for a home visit or bring the child into the baby clinic to be seen if you have any concerns or questions.

Another thing to do is get some breastfeeding support for your partner. The doctor, your hospital or other mothers may be able to recommend a lactation consultant who can come to your home and give hands-on advice to your partner. There may be a branch of La Leche nearby that your partner can contact. *La leche* is Spanish for 'the milk', and the women of La Leche are all dedicated breastfeeding advocates who will do whatever it takes to help a struggling new mother. The NCT also has dedicated breastfeeding counsellors and a telephone helpline.

Try these organizations for help with breastfeeding:

· La Leche League (www.laleche.org.uk); 24-hour helpline 0845 120 2918.
· The National Childbirth Trust (www.nctpregnancyandbabycare.com); breastfeeding helpline 0870 444 8708.

Reservations about Breastfeeding

Some men do not want their partner to breastfeed. They worry that the baby's constant tugging on her breasts will make them droop and sag. They want to resume normal lovemaking as soon as they can, and they feel that breastfeeding might somehow get in the way. They may also feel left out of the tight bond formed by a mother and her nursing child.

Some women do not want to breastfeed. They may not want to in part because their partner has made his feelings known that he doesn't like it. Many women prefer to bottle-feed their babies from the beginning and not worry about things such as their breasts leaking milk on a new silk blouse. Some people are embarrassed by the sight of a woman nursing.

If you or your partner falls into any of these categories, you still might want to give breastfeeding a try just to see how it works. Even one month of receiving his mother's milk will produce priceless health benefits for your child. If you have to go to formula after that, well, at least you know you and your partner did the best you could.

If you and your partner choose to supplement your baby's diet with infant formula, you can, as the child's father, participate in feedings yourself. Giving your baby a bottle will supply her with nourishment, build a bond between the two of you and provide your partner and her sore breasts with a much-needed break.

Helping Out Around the House

When your partner was pregnant, you probably found yourself doing more around the house. With the baby at home, you can expect this trend to continue. You are going to be doing more of everything. Even if you work, even if you are away for eight to ten hours a day at a job, you can expect this. Because as soon as you return home, you will have to pitch in with the baby and everything else that needs to be done.

You and your partner can drive yourselves mad trying to keep an immaculate house while caring for the baby, or you can adopt what is called the 'good-enough rule'. This rule means exactly that – it's good enough. You can live with it, whatever it is, and that is fine for the moment. If something in the house falls below the good-enough standard, that is when you know you need to focus on it.

What if 'good enough' isn't acceptable to my partner?
Talk to her about it. She may simply have a different definition of what's 'good enough'. Remember, too, that she will have her hands full with the baby during the day and may not be able to clean or cook dinner while you are away at work.

The good-enough rule is a survival tactic and a way to keep your sanity. With a newborn in the house, you and your partner are simply not going to be able to devote as much time as you normally do to cooking, cleaning and other household matters. You need to preserve your energy and mental resources for your number-one job – taking care of your constantly demanding, unrelenting baby.

Caring for Your Child

There are lots of ways to care for your child. One is to go to work, bring home a pay cheque and help to support your family financially. Many new fathers work overtime or take a second job to provide more for their family during this time.

Another way to support your child is by supporting your partner. Her attention will be focused on the baby. By helping your partner – by encouraging her with breastfeeding, if she chooses to do this, by pitching in with the housework and cooking the meals, by taking the baby for a while so she can get a much-deserved rest – you are helping your child. The bond established between mother and child is the engine that drives early childhood development, and it is a father's job to promote this special connection.

Mum Gets in the Way

Assisting your partner, so as to promote the bond between her and her child, is only one part of your job, however. The other part – establishing your own connection – may not be quite as obvious. Surprisingly perhaps, in many relationships, the person who often interferes with your doing this is your partner.

She is going to spend lots more time with the baby than you are. If she breastfeeds, for example, the baby is going to be with her for long periods off and on throughout the day and night. While she is at home with the baby, you are going to be at work. She will almost certainly become the expert in the family on all things related to the baby, such as feeding him, taking him to the doctor, overseeing his nap routine and so forth.

In addition, whenever she gets the chance and has the energy, she will probably be reading books and magazines about babies and childhood development, visiting parenting websites, talking to her mother and her friends on the phone and making connections with other mothers of newborns. She is motivated to learn everything she can because she wants to take good care of her child.

All this is wonderful for the most part, but the mother's natural dominance in all areas having to do with the baby can sometimes nudge the father onto the sidelines. This can make him feel like an observer in his own family.

One of the chief ways that fathers interact with their children is through play. While children tend to look to their mothers for comfort, they turn to their fathers for stimulation – activity, playfulness, wrestling. Even a baby will respond differently to his mother than his father, becoming more animated in his father's presence.

Mum and Dad Interaction

Because Mum is the expert and most familiar with the baby, she sometimes shows little or no patience with Dad, who is not as experienced in changing nappies or burping the baby and doesn't quite do it right – or at least not the way Mum likes it to be done. Dad feels criticized or inadequate, and he pulls back from baby-related responsibilities, thus creating a void that Mum needs to fill. She starts doing even more of the baby stuff than she already has been, while Dad goes out to the shed to tinker with his power tools.

Sometimes men are quite happy to abdicate their childrearing responsibilities. Their partner wants to do it? Great. Let her do it. Even if she doesn't want to do it all the time, some men know that their partners will cover for them with the baby if they get out to go fishing or play golf or go out for a pint after work.

Problems can develop in a relationship, however, if either the man or the woman is continually pushing off the child responsibilities onto the other parent. That vital father–child connection – which is just as vital, in its own way, as the mother–child connection – is inevitably going to be weaker and more tentative.

You may need to gently explain to your partner that she can help improve the father–child relationship by taking a well-deserved break now and then. Let the two of you – you and the baby – work things out by yourselves for a while. And really give it a try. If you keep asking her for help when it is your time with the baby, your partner won't learn to relax and let go.

Jobs You Can Do

Taking care of a newborn is not rocket science. When she's hungry, you feed her. If she's breastfeeding, hand her to your partner. If her diet needs to be supplemented with formula, give her a bottle. To whip up a batch of formula, follow the instructions on the label to the letter.

When a baby's nappies are wet or dirty, change them. To a non-parent, changing nappies may seem like the most complicated thing in the world. When you become a parent, it quickly becomes second nature because you are changing nappies all the time.

When the baby's fretful, pick her up and walk around with her. Sometimes taking her outside into the fresh air can settle her down. A baby sling – Baby Bjorn is a popular brand – will hold the baby close to your chest and let you keep your hands free.

At night, when the baby cries, get her and bring her back to bed. (Assuming, of course, she is not already in bed with you.) Your partner can feed her from there. Baby still may need to be comforted. Walk her around the living room until she falls asleep.

One of the coolest things you will ever do in your entire life is fall asleep with your newborn in your arms. There is nothing like it in the world. You are on the sofa watching the match, and she is lying on your chest, snoozing away. Slowly but surely your eyelids grow heavy, and before you know it, the two of you are gently snoring away together. Meanwhile, in another part of the home, your partner is taking a break or resting herself.

The amount of time fathers spend with their children continues to increase. In 1997, fathers spent 23 hours per week with their children, up from 19 hours in the early 1980s. Mothers, on the other hand, spent less time with their children over the same period – 31 hours per week in the 1980s, down to 25 hours in 1997.

Getting Rest

Adequate rest is essential for a newborn. It is also essential for her parents. The trouble is, rest is hard to come by because a newborn may only sleep for two to three hours at a time, if that. She is on her own wake-and-sleep routine, and she couldn't care less about the fact that you have to get up in the morning to go to work.

It is easy to pick out a new father or new mother at the office. New parents look as if they haven't had a good night's sleep in weeks because, well, they haven't. Their eyes are bloodshot, their hair is frazzled, their skin is a sickly pale. They look like zombies because they do what zombies do: stagger around in the dark of night. While the rest of the world sleeps, they are groggily awake, tending to the baby.

You and your partner will need to work out a routine so that both of you get the rest you need. Maybe she takes most or all of the late-night wake-ups during the week, letting you sleep because of your job. Then, maybe before you go to work, you take the baby in the early morning, allowing her to sleep in a little longer. Perhaps you reverse this rhythm at the weekends.

You will obviously have more flexibility at weekends and on your days off. One suggestion might be that you take the baby, say, every Saturday morning. Make it a regular deal. Your partner can sleep in and do whatever she wants. This will provide a boost to her spirits, and give her something to look forward to each week.

Emotional Highs and Lows

Bringing a newborn home for the first time is an emotional moment, bringing happiness and joy. Your home and your life are filled in a way they never were before. You never knew how much you could love a person until you met this child.

Nevertheless, this is also a hectic, emotionally draining and demanding time. Neither you nor your partner is getting enough rest. The baby is like a dictator and you are his servants, constantly jumping to cater to his every whim and need. You are under a lot of stress, and as a result, you may feel an assortment of emotions other than pure bliss and gratitude.

The Baby Blues

Your partner may become depressed, seemingly for no reason at all. 'Wait a second', you say. 'You've got the baby you've always dreamed of. Now you're miserable?' It may not make sense logically, but it still happens with many women. The technical name for it is postpartum depression – commonly known as 'the baby blues'.

There are a number of reasons for your partner to become depressed. It may be hormonal. Her body has been putting her through the wringer for the past nine months – tending to a newborn is like one more turn of the screw. In addition, she is recovering physically from the rigours of labour and delivery, and this will take many months.

Staying at home with her newborn may be what she always wanted. But she may find that the reality of it is not what she dreamed of. Caring for a newborn can be isolating, confining and frustrating. If she is breastfeeding, she is always on demand, and she may feel as if she never gets a moment to herself. She may push herself to exhaustion, even as she worries about her baby and neglects herself.

In extreme cases, postpartum depression can be serious. It is possible that your partner may need professional therapy. While she is breastfeeding, however, she should avoid taking antidepressants. Generally speaking, whatever she ingests will appear in a diluted form in her breast milk.

With you at work much of the time, you may need to recruit some reinforcements to help your partner with the baby. Perhaps one of her family members or a paid helper can come into the house once or twice a week. Some communities also have new mother support groups or mother's clubs. Joining a La Leche group may help as well, since she will meet other women whose experience is similar.

Most importantly, you need to stay in tune with what's going on with her. All she may need is to know that she's not alone in all of this. Give her a chance to express her feelings. After spending all day with the baby, being able to talk to you – another adult – will be a welcome break.

Dad's Blues

So Mum is not feeling all that keen, and guess what? To be honest, you've had better days, too. You're feeling just as overwhelmed and frazzled. You feel as if you're being pulled in all directions at once, with demands coming at you non-stop from the baby, your partner and your job.

The supportive father and husband is supposed to help out at home, but money is tight and he needs to be at work. But when he's at work, he's tired all the time and may be a little distracted. Although he likes to work and wants to be there, he would also like to spend more time with his family. No wonder new fathers get depressed sometimes.

If you're a new father or about to become one, count on being a little overwhelmed at times. But the advice for you is the same as it is for your partner. Get rest and exercise. Find a way to take breaks now and then from your many new responsibilities. And get help if you need it.

Think of all you have done and are doing. You have jumped into this completely new experience with both feet, holding the baby, consoling him when he cries, walking him, feeding him, changing his nappies and putting him down for a nap. All of this is helping to forge a strong connection between the two of you, which he needs and which is good for you, too. This time you are spending with your child provides a big boost for your partner as well, giving her peace of mind and needed breaks. And, amidst the fatigue and swirling emotions of this time, you are still able to experience, with your new family, moments of pure joy.

Chapter 20

What's Ahead for You and Your Family

And so it begins. You and your partner have brought your baby home and somehow survived the first week. But what happens next? What will the next weeks and months bring? This chapter explores the work-family balance, child care, the constant pressures of time and money, and other issues you will face.

Surviving the First Months

In his Nobel Prize acceptance speech, the American novelist William Faulkner said that he believed that man was destined not just to survive, but to prevail. Faulkner was clearly not talking about new parents coping with a baby in the house. Prevail? Forget about it! All you can hope to do is survive.

The first days and weeks and months with a newborn are going to be chaotic. Oh, come on, let's at least be honest. It is not just a matter of days, weeks and months. It will take years before you regain the equilibrium you lost when that sweet, innocent, cuddly baby entered your lives and knocked you off your feet.

Because of the demands the baby will make on you, you will have less time for everything. You will get less sleep. You will have even less sex. Amidst the craziness, though, there will be moments of pure sweetness with your child and your partner. And then, after these amazing, wonderful moments pass, you will return to the general craziness of life.

The Work–Family Balance

You may have been one of the lucky fathers who was able to take a week or two (or longer) to stay home after the baby was born. You experienced firsthand what it was like to take care of a newborn full-time. Thanks to this episode of pure chaos, you felt even luckier to be able to resume your regular schedule and return to the relative sanity of your job.

Immediately, though, a new issue in your life reared its head – the work–family balance. You have dealt with this issue before, juggling the demands of work with your desire to spend time with your partner, but that was nothing like this. Having a baby adds a whole new level of stress to the balancing act.

More Demands at Home

The first thing you realize is that with a baby, there are many more demands at home. Expect this to continue for the foreseeable future. Your partner is devoting herself full-time to the baby. While you may think that this should be enough, and that she should be able to handle all the duties all by herself, it is going to be too much for her alone. She needs your help.

Expect to receive more calls from her while you're at work. Something has come up with the baby, and she needs to talk to you about it. When you phone home to see how things are going, you can almost count on her sounding overwhelmed and exhausted. Gradually she will develop a routine and a nap schedule for the baby that allows her to get breaks during the day, but this will take time.

You may phone your partner on some days and only hear a litany of complaints — how tired she is, how fretful the baby is, how she cannot get five minutes to herself. Let her talk (as much as you can during work) because this will make her feel better. All she may need is to have an adult conversation for a few minutes.

More Demands at Work

While the demands at home have increased with the arrival of a baby, your work schedule has become crazier as well. If your work allows it, and you can afford it, you may want to go back to work initially on a part-time basis. Perhaps for a couple of weeks you can find a way to reduce your hours spent at work in order to spend more time at home. Most new fathers, however, go back full-time, partly because their employer expects and demands it and partly because they need the money.

Men want and need to be working because that is how they can best support their family at this time. Mum is taking care of baby in the nest, and you're making sure there is a nest for them to be in.

Due to the money pressures, many new fathers put in more hours on the job. While this helps out with the finances, it can put a strain on your home life. You may feel torn between being home with your new family and your desire and need to be a success at work.

Exploring Other Options

In most families, the man tends to make more money than the woman. But this is not uniformly true. In an increasing number of families today, the woman is the chief bread-winner. This may result in a different sort of family dynamic – one where Mum goes off to work, while Dad stays home with the baby.

In the first few months, especially if Mum is breastfeeding, it is going to be hard for her to leave the baby. She is also recovering physically from childbirth, which can take quite a while. But many new mothers can and do return to full-time work as early as six weeks to two months after giving birth.

Stay-at-Home Dad

Economics are the biggest reason that some fathers stay home with their children while their partners work outside the house. But money is not the only reason. Lots of men enjoy spending time with their kids and are not averse to the idea of 'downsizing' their lives in order to be their children's primary carer.

In some families, the couple makes a bargain. If she earns more money, she agrees to work for a number of years to allow him to go back to college or receive more training in his profession. The higher level of training or schooling will give him the opportunity to get a better job with higher pay. When he is ready, he re-enters the job market and returns the favour to his partner. Now she has her chance to ease off on her workload and spend more time with the children, if she so chooses.

But this is certainly not always the case with stay-at-home dads and work-outside-the-house mums. In some families, it just works better that way. Dad is the one who does the heavy lifting with baby, putting him down for a nap, feeding him when he wakes up, burping him, changing him, walking him around in a baby sling and later a buggy, and taking him to the park to be with the other babies and parents.

Dad Support

While many stay-at-home dads enjoy this role, they represent only a small minority of fathers. For proof of this, all you have to do is take your baby to the park on a weekday afternoon. There, you will find mainly mothers with their children.

It is different at weekends. Then, when the men are home from work, they take their children to the park to give their partners a break. But during the week you can still see that the traditional roles apply. Mum (and a grandparent, here and there) is usually tending to the children, while Dad is off at work.

Recent research indicates that around 155,000 men in the UK stay at home to look after the home and family. Some are 'house-husbands' at home full-time; others work part-time and share the childcare, or are bringing up children by themselves. If you are one of them, then you could get in touch with HomeDad UK (www.homedad.org.uk), a support group dedicated to helping dads at home with their children.

Feeling outnumbered, many stay-at-home dads feel the need to link up with other men in their situation – if they can find them – and form a support group. This is not a bad idea for new fathers in general. The demands on you at this time are so intense that you may feel the need to talk to other men who are in the same boat you are.

Check out your local hospital or community centre. It may sponsor a monthly group session in which new dads – both those who have full-time jobs and the fathers who stay at home with their children – get together with other new dads and bring their babies. Not only do you get to connect with other men, you spend some time with your child. Chat rooms on websites devoted to parenting are another way in which you can hook up with new fathers and form a virtual community.

Finding Childcare

Once your partner starts back to work, and perhaps even before this occurs, the biggest issue you will face is finding childcare. In most families, Mum takes the lead in this area, visiting nurseries and interviewing childminders to find the right situation. She will need to talk to you about what she has found, and you may need to visit one or two of the places and talk to the people there to help you both come to a final decision.

Basically, there are three options for childcare. One is in-home care, in which a nanny or a babysitter comes into your house and watches your child on a one-on-one basis. The second type is a childminder, in which your child stays in the home of a licensed provider while you are at work. The third type is a day nursery, which is a more formal environment than a person's home and usually has a routine similar to a preschool. With both nurseries and childminders, the provider will also be supervising other children, in addition to your own.

Some childcare providers will not accept a baby who is younger than three months old. Childcare is expensive (a nanny being the most expensive option). The younger the child, the more expensive it will be. Babies need to be held virtually all the time, and they need continual attention. Childcare providers will charge accordingly for this service.

Many parents rely on family members to help them out with childcare. If the baby's grandparents live nearby and are willing to watch your child, that will save you a considerable amount of money. In addition, they may really enjoy developing a close relationship with their grandchild. In the long run, though, you will probably need to rely not just on family but on a permanent solution to the childcare issue. Your family will be able to help you out when they can, but you need to find somebody you can count on every day of the working week.

Be careful how you handle the babysitting issue with the child's grandparents. If you rely on them too much, they may feel that you're taking them for granted. Make sure you acknowledge their contributions and thank them for all they're doing.

Overall, your childcare provider must be a caring person who is experienced with children and good with them, with the ability and desire to establish a good rapport with your child. She needs to be dependable, safe, clean, well versed in basic first aid and resuscitation, aware of what to do in an emergency, and be licensed. You and your partner should feel confident that your provider is going to take care of your child as if she were her own. Life will be unsettled and chaotic until you find the right childcare provider. Once you do, things will become much smoother.

The Battle for Sleep

It is well known that one of the most effective means of torturing people is through sleep deprivation. This method is used, for instance, by combatants during wartime. To obtain information from a reluctant-to-talk prisoner of war, interrogators change and disrupt his sleep schedule, turning day into night and night into day. He becomes disorientated and more dependent on his captors and, it is thought, more willing to spill the beans to them.

As the father of a newborn, you may feel a little like a prisoner of war being subjected to sleep deprivation techniques. You stagger around bleary-eyed and yawning uncontrollably. By the middle of the afternoon, you feel like crawling under your desk for a long nap. Sleep for a new father is like sex – you are simply not going to get enough of it.

Baby's Sleep Schedule

One of your prime goals as a new parent will be to get your baby on the same sleep routine as yours. In other words, you want her to sleep through the night with no wake-ups. Realistically, though, you and your partner are going to have to endure many sleep-interrupted nights before your child reaches this point.

Some babies begin to sleep through the night almost immediately. You always hate to talk to these parents if you are a new parent and your child wakes up frequently. It is impossible not to feel jealous. These people are bright-eyed, with lots of energy, while you're struggling to keep your eyes open after having woken three times in the middle of the night by your squalling baby.

Nevertheless, you ask them how they did it – how they achieved this miracle of a baby sleeping through the night – and they tell you what works for them. Unfortunately, what worked for them may not work for you. Here are some of the issues that are involved in teaching a baby to sleep through the night:

· The age of the baby.
· Her daily routine.
· When she takes her naps.
· How long her naps are.
· What the baby eats, and how often.
· Where the baby sleeps (in her bed or with parents).
· Whether her parents help her to sleep by rocking or by other methods.

Generally, by about six months, babies begin to sleep through the night. But not always. As with so many things having to do with babies, much of this depends on the child. Some babies sleep as contentedly as cats, while others are more restless and stir more often.

Keeping a consistent routine is a vital ingredient in helping teach your baby how to sleep through the night. She needs to do basically the same things at roughly the same time each day. This includes her nighttime schedule. Habit and routine can help teach her when it is time to go to sleep.

Your Sleep Schedule (and Your Partner's)

Doctors and parenting experts like to advise new parents to sleep when their baby sleeps. If the baby is only sleeping for two hours at a time, be sure to get some rest at those times, even if this means stopping in the middle of doing something. Once the baby wakes up, you are going to be on demand again. If you do not rest when you get the chance, you are going to drive yourself to exhaustion and possibly depression.

Your best ally in this regard is your partner, just as you are her best ally. Find an arrangement that works for both of you. If you have to get up in the morning to go to work, let her take the night shift with the baby during the week. On the weekends, reverse roles. You need to exchange duties with the baby so each of you can get breaks and sleep.

If you need to work and cannot get the sleep you need, you may want to consider staying one night a week at a friend's or your parents' house, if they live nearby. Your overtired partner may also want to consider doing the same – just to get a good night's rest.

Time and Money Pressures

Parents of newborns are under a lot of pressure. The needs of the baby are nearly constant. He is vulnerable and helpless and cannot use words yet to tell you what he likes or dislikes. Sometimes he falls ill and needs to go to the doctor. Meanwhile, you must deal with the worries and handle all the responsibilities while you're feeling stressed and completely worn out from a lack of sleep.

Adding to these pressures are those two old regulars, not enough money and a lack of time. You never had enough money or time before. Now, with a child, your wallet and calendar seem stretched almost to the breaking point. To find a way to handle all your added responsibilities, you will likely need to cut back temporarily on certain things you used to do regularly, such as getting together with friends after work. When life takes on a more normal shape again, you can resume those activities.

As long as you have a young child (or children), there will be demands on your time and wallet. If you can, however, take a longer view. Gradually, the seemingly overwhelming responsibilities that you currently feel will ease up. The yoke will lighten. The first year of your baby's life is probably the most harried you will ever feel as a parent. Rest assured that one of these days, you will get your life back.

You and Your Partner

It is a sad fact of life that many of the fathers who are reading this book will have a longer relationship with their child than they will with the child's mother. Everybody knows the unhappy statistics. One in three marriages ends in divorce. 25 per cent of these divorced couples have children under five.

In most of these families, the children will live with the mother, who will retain custody. But in a number of households, the father keeps custody and is the primary caretaker of the children.

Single Fathers with Children

Without a doubt, many single fathers never expected to be the primary caretakers of their children. Perhaps they went into their marriages or relationships thinking that theirs would be a traditional arrangement, in which the woman handled the bulk of the childrearing duties. Then circumstances changed for them, and they became the custodial parents.

Many of these men may not have bothered to read a book like this, because they felt it would never apply to them. Their wives would handle it all. Now they find themselves doing all the things that single mothers must routinely do: changing all the nappies, cooking the meals, reading the bedtime story, putting their child down at night, taking her to and from day care and school, and all the rest of it.

A Job Meant for Two

Most single dads do a terrific job. So do most single mums. And they may be grateful they're finished with their former spouses, because the relationship just wasn't working. It wasn't working for them, and the constant squabbling seemed to be hurting the children, too.

Even so, if you can avoid it – and most single mums and dads would agree with this – you do not want to go down that road. Parenting is a job best suited for two. Furthermore, the best gift you can give your child is to have a healthy, loving relationship with your partner.

Keeping Your Relationship Vibrant

Babies put stress on a relationship. You will not have as much time with your partner as you used to. When you do find time to be together without the baby, both of you are likely to be tired and stressed from all your other responsibilities.

If you do not want to go down the painful road of separation and divorce (and you do not), you need to find ways to keep your relationship with your partner living and vibrant. That does not necessarily mean taking week-long romantic getaways to the Mediterranean, although those are nice. Rather, it means making small connections with your partner every day. That might mean any of the following:

· Walking together with the baby.
· Talking about the baby, but not *only* about the baby.
· Going shopping or doing other mundane errands together, just to spend time with your partner.
· Holding her hand or rubbing her shoulders, for no specific reason.
· Surprising her with flowers or a gift.
· Going out together (without the baby) from time to time.
· Cuddling in bed at the end of the day.

Sex will return. Not right away – it will take at least six weeks after the baby is born, and probably longer, before your partner is likely to be ready – and probably not as frequently as before. But gradually, as your partner begins to feel better physically and emotionally, you will be able to rediscover this side of your relationship.

Don't push too hard about sex. It will be counterproductive if you do. It takes a long time for many new mothers to feel interested in sex after giving birth. Nor can they relax fully in their still-recuperating bodies. Be a man with a slow hand, as the song goes, and you will be better off.

You and Your Baby

The same advice applies to your relationship with your child as well – take it slowly. You've got your whole life to get to know this child. Don't feel bad if for some reason you do not feel totally connected to your child the moment she is born.

Some parents expect to fall immediately and completely in love with their child the instant they lay eyes on her. This does occur, certainly. But love usually acts less like a lightning bolt and more like a plant. It takes time and care and nurturing to blossom.

It's Mum's Show in the Beginning

In the early days and months of having a baby, it is basically all Mum's show. Now that does not mean that Dad cannot contribute. Of course he can. He can do all the things that Mum does with the baby (except breastfeed, of course), while building his own close relationship with his child.

Having said that, the point still stands. This early time with the baby, with some exceptions, is basically Mum's show. When the baby needs to eat, Mum will mainly feed him. When he needs to settle down, Mum will mainly take him and put him down. She bore this child with her own body, and in most cases she will act as primary caretaker for him in his tender years.

Your Time Is Coming

Most new fathers do not dispute these facts or seek to overturn them. They like the fact that Mum is in charge of the baby. They consider that their principal job is to be good helpers – helping their partners, helping to take care of their children and helping to create an environment in which Mum and baby feel protected and safe.

As a new father, one thing you can look forward to is the future. It keeps getting better. Every day the baby gets older, it gets better for you. The baby grows stronger and livelier and is more able to interact with you – daily, she is emerging from her larva-like state and becoming more of an emerging butterfly. This will give both of you more and more chances to enjoy each other's company.

Men define success in a variety of ways. This might include making money, achieving recognition in their work, earning the admiration of their peers or having a loving relationship with a woman. But nearly 90 per cent of all men say that being a good father is an essential ingredient of a successful life.

Remembering to Enjoy

Because of the influence of television and films, people tend to have an idealized view of family life. Even though their own families were, well, bizarre, they seem to think that other families have to be sane and normal by comparison. In the backs of their minds, they imagine that family life should really be like one of those old black-and-white sitcoms from the early 1960s.

What they find, in actual practice, is that family life doesn't come close to resembling what is depicted in films and on television – even if the new sitcom standard for parents is Homer and Marge Simpson. Family life is messy. It is chaotic. It is a big jumble of struggling people and hurt feelings and dirty nappies and wet sheets and food on the kitchen floor and dogs with fleas and no time to think and emergency visits to the doctor and parents shouting to be heard and babies crying and one brother smacking the other and on and on and on. Given all this, it is a wonder why anyone in his right mind decides to become a parent these days.

But you have, and now you're stuck. And with the baby crying in the next room, you're not going to get much time to enjoy it. So grab those moments of pleasure while you can and cherish each one.

When you become a father, there is so much learn. Finding the right work–family balance can take time. So can finding the right childcare situation, and so can teaching your child to sleep through the night. You must juggle the constant demands on your money and time with the need to maintain a close relationship with your partner and child. Remember to enjoy yourself as much as you can, and you'll do fine.

Appendices

Appendix A

Suggested Reading
for New Fathers

Appendix B

Websites for Fathers

Appendix A

Suggested Reading for New Fathers

Sansom, Ian. *The Truth about Babies.* (Granta).
Not a book of advice, but one father's view.

Berkmann, Marcus. *Fatherhood: The Truth.* (Vermilion).
Contains good advice that succeeds in being truthful and funny at the same time.

Giles, Stephen. *From Lad to Dad (How to Survive as a Pregnant Father).* (White Ladder Press).
Helpful guide, but less jokey than Berkmann.

Smith, Jon. *The Bloke's Guide to Pregnancy.* (Hay House).
Does what it says on the cover.

Hallows, Richard. *Full-Time Father: How to Succeed as a Stay-at-Home Dad.* (White Ladder Press).
Written by a stay-at-home dad, it draws on his own experience and that of other home dads and is a truthful, useful guide.

Hilling, Hogan. *The Man Who Would Be Dad.* (Capital Books).
A deeply personal account dealing with feelings that dads are often afraid to admit to. Also covers his experiences of a stay-at-home dad of three sons from 0–10.

Nilsson, Lennart. *A Child Is Born.* (Bantam Doubleday).
Nilsson's extraordinary photographs depict the growth of an embryo and foetus within the womb. These pictures may help fathers-to-be feel more connected to what is going on inside their partners.

Appendix B

Websites for Fathers

www.babycentre.co.uk

An excellent parenting website for mum and dad. Hundreds of resources, loads of brilliant and reassuring advice.

www.nctpregnancyandbabycare.com

The National Childbirth Trust's site. Sound, trustworthy advice. Easy to navigate.

www.fathersdirect.com

Everything for expectant and new fathers. Its 'New Dads' section is 'especially for all you blokes who are about to, or have just become a father. There's loads of information to help you through it all here.'

www.midwivesonline.com

If you need advice, ask a midwife online on this great site.

www.oneparentfamilies.org.uk

Speaks for itself, really. Very useful site.

www.homedad.org.uk

'Whatever your situation, HomeDad UK is the only UK support group dedicated to helping dads at home with their kids.'

www.dads-uk.co.uk

For dads going through the pain of separation and divorce.

www.nhsdirect.nhs.uk

The website of the NHS. Your medical queries answered online.

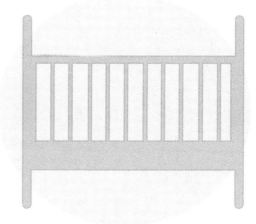

Index

A

Active labour, 179–80
Advice
    from father-in-law, 59
    on finances, 90
    from mother/mother-in-law, 58
    for personal fears, 77–79
    weighing, 78
Advisory role, 8
Air bags, 162
Alcohol, 18, 118–20
    effect on foetus, 119
    sleep safety and, 158
    your role, 119–20, 126
Amniocentesis, 50–51
Announcing newborn, 215–17
Antibiotics, 18
Apgar test, 214–15

B

Babies
    activities of, 225
    caring for, 233–35
    childcare, 243–45
    early months, 240
    enjoying, 251
    future with, 250–51
    introducing pet to, 225–27
    nannies for, 244
    playing with, 234
    sleep schedule, 236, 245–46
Baby blues, 237–38
Baby delivery. See Delivery, of baby;
    Labour
Baby development
    alcohol and, 18, 119, 126
    first trimester, 18, 26, 43
    gender and, 46–48
    heartbeat detection, 43
    kicking, 27–28, 137
    nutrition and. See Nutrition

recreational drugs and, 18,
    121–22
    second trimester, 27–28
    sex and, 134–35
    smoking and, 18, 120
    third trimester, 28
Baby expenses, 89
Baby health tests, 214–15, 218, 227
Babyproofing home, 158–59
Bed, family, 157–58
Birth. See Childbirth; Delivery, of
    baby
Birth partner, 165–76
    active participation, 6–7
    assistance with, 174–76
    baby advocacy and, 167–68
    birth details/plan and, 148–49
    birth team and, 193–195
    caesarean sections, 208–10
    childbirth preparation classes
        and, 167–68
    doulas assisting, 89, 175–76,
        193–194
    emotional support, 169
    home birth vs. hospital and, 148
    hospital logistics and. See
        Hospitals
    overview, 6–7
    pain relief and. See Pain relief
        (partner)
    partner advocacy and, 166–67
    physical support, 168–69
    placenta and, 200–1
    professional assistance, 175–76
    relationship importance, 4
    roles, 4, 6–9, 166–68
    team approach, 186, 193–195
    See also Labour
Birth control, 152–53
Birth defects, detecting, 50–51
Birth plan
    alternatives, 203

developing, 148–49
Birth team, 193–95
    communication, 193–94
    medical side, 194
    non-medical group, 193–94
Blood tests, 16–17
Body changes (partner), 31
    after pregnancy, 133–34
    sex and, 132–34, 139
    weight gain, 33–35
Books, 254
Boy/girl. See Gender (baby)
Braxton Hicks contractions, 28, 181
Breastfeeding, 229–32
    baby blues and, 237–38
    baby weight and, 230–31
    formula supplementing, 231, 235
    La Leche groups, 231, 237
    milk benefits, 219, 230
    partner femininity and, 230
    reservations, 231–32
    support, 218–19, 229–30, 231
Breasts, 31, 35, 206–7
Breech babies, 208
Burn prevention, 160–61

C

Caesarean sections, 209–11
    defined, 209
    emergencies, 210, 211
    neonatal ICU for, 212
    overuse caution, 209
    reasons for, 207–8
    recovery from, 210
    safety of, 207
    statistics, 210
    your role, 209–10, 218
Caffeinated beverages, 18, 123–24
Camcorders, 220–21
Career. See Job/career

Cars
  buying, 94–96
  emergency deliveries in, 213
Car seats, 167–69
  air bags and, 168
  basics, 168
  importance of, 167–68
  installing, 169, 234
Cats, 237
Cervix dilation, 186, 197, 198, 202, 204
Childbirth
  environment, 6
  historical perspective, 5
  at home, 6
  as medical procedure, 5–6
  preparation classes, 174–75
  today, 6
  See also Delivery, of baby; Labour; Unexpected occurrences
Childcare, 253–55
Childproofing home, 163–64
Coffee, 18, 125–26
Communication
  after birth, 244
  announcing newborn, 225–27
  within team, 201–2
  complimenting partner, 35
  confiding in partner, 79
  decisions and. See Decisions
  discussing issues, 6
  during emotional highs/lows, 28, 36–38
  finance discussion, 85, 94, 105–6
  with hospital, 191, 193, 198
  listening and, 4
  mobile phones for, 167, 226–27
  on workplace safety/comfort, 112
Conception
  due date from, 17
  mechanics of, 12
Contractions, 185, 186, 187, 198, 202, 205. See also Labour
Cooking, 127–28
Coping strategies, 63–65
Couvade syndrome, 32

Cravings
  partner, 30–31
  sympathy, 32
Credit card debt, 88–89
Credit counselling, 91
Cribs
  safety, 160, 161–62
  used, 161
Crowning, 206
Cutting cord, 206
CVS (chorionic villus sampling), 50, 51

D
Dad's blues, 238
Decision-making role, 8–9
Decisions, 6, 141–52
  birth control, 149
  birth details/plan, 148, 203
  home birth vs. hospital, 6, 147–48
  naming baby, 143–45
  nappies, 151–52
  nursery decoration, 155–56
  participating in, 142, 148
  on sharing information, 145–46
Delivery, of baby
  announcing, 215–17
  attending consultant and, 40–41, 199
  caesarean sections, 207–10
  celebrating, 221–22
  crowning and, 199
  cutting cord, 199
  emergency roadside, 204
  family time after, 214
  forceps for, 205
  head shape upon, 199
  health tests after, 214–15, 218, 227
  holding baby and, 199–200
  medical interventions, 204–5
  photographing after, 219
  placenta and, 200–1
  seeing newborn, 199

  videotaping, 220–21
  See also Hospitals; Labour; Unexpected occurrences
Depression
  postpartum, 237–38
  from pregnancy news, 13–14
Dilation, 180, 191, 192, 193, 197
Disability benefits, 112, 204
Disaster planning, 161–62
Divorce, 247–48
Dogs, 238
Doulas, 89
  costs, 89, 175
  defined, 175
  function of, 175–76
  medical team and, 193
  supporting role, 176
Downs syndrome, 50
Drugs, 18, 121–22
Due date
  approaching, anxiety, 28
  conception-to-birth time frame, 17
  overdue baby and, 206–7
  revealing or not, 17–18, 146

E
Early labour, 179, 186–87
Education
  making savings, 101–2
  for job change, 116
Effaced cervix, 180, 191
Emergency responses, 159–62
  disaster planning and, 161–62
  infant resuscitation, 160
  overview, 159
Emergency roadside delivery, 204
Emotions
  after birth, 236–38
  baby blues, 237–38
  Dad's blues, 238
  of extended family, 59–60
  gender knowledge and, 47–48
  isolation feeling, 62–63
  miscarriage and, 52–53

of money, 84–86
money and, 70–71
mood swings, 28, 36–38
postpartum depression, 237–38
pregnancy news and, 13–14
providing support, 169
stress and. *See* Stress
twins and, 49–50
Enjoying fatherhood, 251
Epidurals, 167–68, 193, 194, 197.
    See also Pain relief (partner)
Episiotomy, 201
Equipment, 89
Estate planning, 100–101
Excitement, 14
Exercise, 64, 127–28
Expenses, baby, 89

F

Fainting, 4, 30, 68–69
False labour, 171, 181, 186
Family
    accepting help from, 62, 244
    advice from, 58, 59
    announcing newborn to, 215–17
    emotional responses, 20–21,
        59–60
    father, 61
    father-in-law, 58–59
    monetary gifts from, 88
    mother, 58, 60–61
    mother-in-law, 58
    of partner, 57–60
    pregnancy announcement, 19–21
Family bed, 157–58
Family doctors, 40, 41
Father-in-law, 58–59
Father (your)
    anticipating grandparenthood,
        61
    bad role model, 74
    good role model, 74
    influence of, 73–75
Fears, 67–79
    of ageing, 71–73

for baby, 76–77
of being like Dad, 73–75
of fainting, 4, 30, 68–69
of fatherhood duties, 72
financial, 69–71
isolation feeling and, 62–63
of mortality, 72–73
normality of, 68, 73, 83
for partner, 76
of paternity accuracy, 71
from pregnancy news, 13
for relationship, 75–76
sadness/depression and, 13–14
support for, 77–79
See also Stress
Feeding baby, 231, 235. *See also*
    Breastfeeding
Finances
    advice on, 90
    affording time with child, 70,
        108
    baby expenses, 89
    borrowing money, 87–88
    credit card debt, 88–89
    credit counselling, 91
    discussion points, 85, 94, 105–6
    emotions and, 70–71, 84–86
    fears/worries, 69–71, 82–83, 247
    income strategies, 86–89
    mathematical reality, 70
    monetary gifts, 87–88
    planning. *See* Financial planning
    provider role, 3–4
    setting priorities, 86
    as shared responsibility, 83–84
    upbringing and, 84–86
    using existing resources, 87
    your/her viewpoints, 82–83
Financial planning, 93–102
    for baby arrival, 104–6
    buying homes and, 96–98
    education savings and, 101–2
    leadership role, 94
    life insurance and, 98–100
    partner income loss and, 105
    retirement and, 102

vehicles and, 94–96
wills/estates and, 100–101
See also Job/career
Fire prevention, 161
Foetal alcohol syndrome, 119
Food
    aversions, 30, 31
    to avoid, 123
    caffeinated beverages, 18, 123–24
    coffee, 123–24
    cooking, 125–26
    cravings, 30–31
    eating healthily, 34–35, 122–24,
        125–26
    good habits, 124–25
    sympathy cravings, 32
    tea, 123–24
    vitamins/supplements, 18
Forceps, 205
Friends, changes, 57
Furniture, 89
Further education savings, 101–2

G

Gatekeeper role, 218
Gender (baby), 46–48
    announcing, 216
    genetics of, 48
    knowing, decision, 46–47
    reacting to, 47–48
Gifts
    for Mum, 222
    for siblings/baby, 219
Grandparents. *See* Family

H

Handwritten wills, 100
Health, 117–28
    alcohol and, 18, 118–20, 126
    diet and, 34–35, 122–24, 125–26
    exercise and, 64, 127–28
    good habits, 124–25
    recreational drugs and, 18,
        121–22

rest and, 128, 203–4
role model for, 118
smoking and, 18, 120–21
Health tests (baby), 214–15, 218, 227
Heartbeat (baby), 43
Help, from family, 62, 234
High-risk pregnancy, 49, 52, 113,
   193, 208
Holding baby, 199–200
Home
   babyproofing, 158–59
   balancing priorities, 98, 240–41
   buying, 96–98
   family bed, 157–58
   increasing demands, 241
   as nest, 97, 154
   nursery preparation, 155–56
   safety. See Safety
   working at, 116–18
Home births, 6, 147–48
Homecoming, 223, 225–38
   baby actions and, 226
   communicating after, 234
   housekeeping and, 232
   pets and, 226–28
   postpartum depression and,
      237–38
   support role, 228–29, 232,
      233–35
Home insurance, 161
Home pregnancy tests, 15–16
Hormone changes
   hers, 26, 29, 30, 36, 131
   his, 32
Hospitals
   admission, 171, 190–91
   attending consultant and, 40–41,
      193
   birth team, 193–94
   checking in, 190–91, 192
   communicating with, 185, 187,
      192
   complaints against, 147
   delivery room procedures,
      192–194

doulas and, 89, 175–76, 193–94
driving to, 185, 187–88
false labour and, 171, 181, 186
home birth vs., 6, 147–48
identification bracelets, 215
items checklist for, 172–73
labour/delivery rooms, 171,
   193–94
length of stay, 222, 223
logistics in, 170–71
neonatal ICU, 171, 210, 218
nurse activities, 192–93, 195
nurseries, 172
'rooming in', 222–23
sent home from, 191–92
taking Mum/baby home, 223
tour of, 170–72, 190
trip preparation, 185
wheelchair use, 170–71
See also Prenatal care
Housekeeping, 232

I
Infant resuscitation, 160
In-laws. See Family
Instincts, trusting, 211
Insurance
   home, 161
   life, 98–100
Internet resources, 2, 255
Isolation feelings, 62–63

J
Job/career, 10, 103–18
   action steps, 106–7
   balancing, 240–41
   changing, 115–16
   creative schedule options, 111,
      242–43
   dissatisfaction, 114–16
   education for, 116
   flexibility, 109–11, 118
   home office, 116–18

improving, 115–16
increasing demands, 241
job sharing, 111
of partner, 112–13
part-time, 111
paternity leave, 108–9
pregnancy policies, 22
reducing work time, 111
sabbaticals, 111
self-employment, 23, 116–18
sharing pregnancy news, 21–23,
   107
stay-at-home dads and, 242–43
telecommuting, 111
time off, 107–11
travel, 10, 113
unemployment and, 117
Jokes (about partner), 31

K
Kicking (of baby), 27–28, 137

L
Labour
   active, 179–80
   Braxton Hicks contractions and,
      28, 181
   cervix dilation and, 180, 191,
      192, 193, 197
   contractions, 179, 180, 181, 192,
      195, 198
   crowning and, 199
   early, 179, 186–87
   early progress signs, 181–82
   empathizing with, 168
   false labour and, 171, 181, 186
   inducing, 178–79, 182, 193, 206–7
   maintaining, 182–83
   monitoring during, 193
   pain relief. See Pain relief
      (partner)
   placenta and, 202–3
   premature, 172, 203–4

pushing and, 180, 181, 197–98
rest and, 184–85, 192
show and, 181
stages, 179–81
stalling, 195–96
transition, 180–81
waters breaking and, 182
your duties, 182–86
See also Delivery, of baby;
    Unexpected occurrences
La Leche groups, 231, 237
Life insurance, 98–100
    mortality and, 72–73, 98–99
    for partner, 99
    term policies, 99–100
Listening, to partner, 4

M

Midwives, 41, 89, 176. *See also*
    Doulas
Miscarriage, 51–53
    amnio/CVS risk, 51
    causes, 51
    emotional toll, 52–53
    sex and, 52
    threat, 51–52
    trying again after, 53
    warning signs, 52
Mobile phones, 161, 216–17
Money. *See* Finances
Mood swings. *See* Emotions
Morning sickness, 27, 29–30, 37,
    131
Mortality
    fears, 72–73, 98–99
    life insurance and, 98–100
Moses baskets, 156, 157
Mother, 58, 60–61
Mother-in-law, 58

N

Naming baby
    after yourself, 145
    common names, 144

considerations, 143–45
    family input, 144
    sharing information on, 146
Nannies, 244
Nappies, 151–52
Natural childbirth, 193, 197
Neonatal intensive care unit (ICU),
    172, 210, 218
Nesting instinct, 97, 154
Normal births, 204–5
Nursery (home), 155–56
Nursery (hospital), 172
Nurses, 192–93, 195
Nutrition
    eating healthily, 34–35, 122–24,
        125–26
    good habits, 124–25
    vitamins/supplements, 18
    See also Food

O

Obstetricians, 40–42
    attending physician and, 40–41,
        193
    relationship with, 41–42
    See also Prenatal care
Overdue baby, 206–7
Oxytocin, 193, 207

P

Pain relief (partner)
    analgesics, 197
    baby welfare and, 167–68
    decisions, 194–95
    drugs, 193, 197
    early labour, 168–69
    epidurals, 167–68, 193, 196, 197
    natural childbirth and, 193, 197
    options, 196–97
    your role, 167–68, 169
Participant role, 4
Partner
    attraction reasons, 86
    baby blues, 237–38

body changes, 31, 33–35, 132–34,
    139
concerns about, 76
disability benefits, 112, 204
divorce from, 247–48
exercise, 127–28
family of, 57–60
gift for, 222
job/career, 105, 112–13, 242
life insurance, 99
losing income of, 105
mood swings, 28, 36–38
peeing urge, 28
postpartum depression and,
    237–38
rest for, 130, 204, 235, 236, 245,
    246–47
social world changes, 56
weight, 33–35
Part-time work, 111
Paternity doubts, 71
Paternity leave, 108–9
Peeing (partner), 28
Pets
    cats, 227
    dogs, 228
    introducing baby to, 226–28
Photographs, 219. *See also*
    Camcorders
Placenta, 200–1
Plan, birth. *See* Birth plan
Planned pregnancy, 12
Positive thinking, 65
Postpartum depression, 237–38
Pregnancy
    blood test, 16–17
    conception and, 12
    due date and, 17–18
    emotional responses, 13–14, 15
    emotional volatility, 36–38
    high-risk, 49, 52, 113, 193, 208
    home tests, 15–16
    initial tasks, 18–19
    learning about, 12–14
    length of, 17
    miscarriage threat, 51–53

morning sickness, 27, 29–30, 37, 131

planned, 12

reacting to, 14–15, 17

reassuring her, 14–15

stages. *See* Pregnancy stages

telling about, 19–23, 51–52

unplanned, 12

weight gain, 33–35

Pregnancy stages, 26–28

first trimester, 26–27

second (middle) trimester, 27–28

third trimester, 28

Premature births

causes, 203–4

increasing rate of, 204

neonatal ICU for, 172

preventing, 204

serious nature of, 204

Prenatal care

amniocentesis, 50–51

attending consultant and, 40–41

birth defects and, 50–51

checkups, 42–43

current state of, 40

CVS, 50, 51

detecting problems, 50–51

family physicians, 40, 41

midwives, 41, 89, 176

obstetricians, 40–42

overview, 40

seeking advice, 30

selecting, 6

tests, 43–44

twins and, 49

ultrasound tests, 40, 44–46, 49

See also Hospitals

Professional therapy, 78–79

Provider/Protector role, 3–4, 233

fears arising, 69–71

as priority, 83, 104

women attracted to, 86

See also Job/career

Pushing (in labour), 180, 181, 197–98

R

Reading suggestions, 254

Recreational drugs, 18, 121–22

Relationship (with partner)

changes, 9–10, 75–76

divorce, 247–48

fears, 75–76

keeping vibrant, 249

Resources

books, 254

Internet, 2, 255

options, 2–3

Responsibilities, 3–4. *See also specific responsibilities*

Rest

avoiding premature births, 204

for baby, 236, 245–46

battle for, 245–47

health and, 128, 204

labour and, 184–85, 192

for new parents, 235, 236, 245, 246–47

for partner, 128, 204, 235, 236, 245, 246–47

Resuscitation, for infants, 160

Retirement planning, 102

Role model(s)

you as, 118

your parents as, 73–75

Roles

advisory, 8

decision-making, 8–9

gatekeeper, 218

initial pregnancy, 18–19

provider/protector, 3–4

supporting. *See* Support role

See also Birth partner

S

Sabbaticals, 111

Sadness, 13–14

Safety

alcohol, sleeping and, 157

babyproofing home, 157–58

burn prevention, 160–61

car seats and, 161–63

of crib, 156, 157

disaster planning, 161

emergency responses, 159–60

of family bed, 158

fire prevention, 161

hospital drive, 185, 187–88

infant resuscitation, 160

mobile phones and, 161

nursery design and, 155

Sex, 129–39

affecting baby, 134–35

after birth, 249

body changes and, 31, 35, 132–34, 139

changing desires, 9, 131, 132, 139

comfortable positions, 137–39

common worries, 135

cuddling/holding and, 136–37

in final two months, 135

foreplay importance, 136

intercourse alternatives, 138–39

intimacy and, 139

miscarriage and, 52

oral, 138–39

overdue baby and, 207

overview, 130

partner as mum and, 133

partner perspective, 130–32, 136–37, 138

during pregnancy, 133–34

pregnancy stage and, 131

second trimester and, 27, 131

Sharing pregnancy news, 19–23, 146

with friends/family, 19–20, 51–52

surprise reactions, 20–21

at work, 21–23

Show, 181

Siblings, meeting baby, 219

Single dads, 248–49

Sleep. *See* Rest

Smoking, 18, 120–21

Social world changes, 56–61

friends, 57

her family, 57–60
of partner, 56
your family, 60–61
Sonography. *See* Ultrasound tests
Spina bifida, 30
Stay-at-home dads, 242–43
Stomach discomfort (male), 32–33
Stress
 after birth, 236–38
 coping strategies, 63–65
 financial advice/counselling,
  90–91
 financial pressures, 69–71, 82–83,
  247
 isolation feeling, 62–63
 postpartum depression, 237–38
 professional help, 78–79
 on relationship, 249
 stay-at-home dads, 243
 support mechanisms, 77–79
 time pressures, 247
Support groups, 78
Support role, 4, 8
 breastfeeding, 218–19, 229–30,
  231
 emotional support, 169
 her changing body and, 31,
  33–35
 homecoming, 228–29, 232,
  233–35
 jokes and, 31
 listening and, 4
 physical support, 168–69
 See also Birth coaching
Sympathy pains, 32–33

T
Telecommuting, 111
Tests
 Apgar, 214–15
 baby health, 214–15, 218, 227
 for pregnancy, 15–17
 prenatal, 43–44
Time, with family (children)
 average, 104

earnings and, 70, 108
ongoing/future, 250–51
pressures, 247
Time pressures, 247
Trimesters, 26–28
 defined, 26
 first, 26–27
 second (middle), 27–28
 third, 28
 See also Baby development
Trusting instincts, 211
Twins, 49–50

U
Ultrasound tests, 40, 44–46
 baby gender and, 46–48
 description, 44–45
 experiencing, 45–46
 function of, 45
 twins and, 49–50
Umbilical cord, 199
Unemployed fathers, 117
Unexpected occurrences
 caesarean sections, 207–10, 218
 emergency roadside delivery, 204
 expecting, 202–3
 flexibility and, 202–3
 medical interventions, 204–5
 overdue baby, 206–7
 premature births, 172, 203–4
 trusting instincts, 211
Unplanned pregnancy, 12

V
Vehicles. *See* Cars
Videotaping birth, 220–21

W
Waterbeds, 158
Waters breaking, 182
Websites, 255
Weight gain (partner), 33–35,
 132–34

Weight (of baby), 216, 230–31
Wheelchairs, 170–71
Wife. *See* Partner
Wills/estate planning, 100–101
World view changes, 10, 55
 coping strategies, 63–65
 family and. *See* Family
 feeling isolated, 62–63
 social world, 56–61
Worries. *See* Fears